NO GIMMICKS

RELEVANCY, COMMITMENT AND EXCELLENCE IN FOUR DECADES OF WORSHIP MINISTRY

D1218388

GODZCHILD PUBLICATIONS

Published by Godzchild Publications
a division of Godzchild, Inc.
22 Halleck St., Newark, NJ 07104
www.godzchildproductions.net

Printed in the United States of America 2016 - First Edition

Library of Congress Cataloging-in-Publications Data
No Gimmicks: Relevancy, Commitment and Excellence in Four Decades of Worship Ministry/Leo Davis

ISBN   978-1-942705-24-6 (pbk.)

1. Davis, Leo. 2. Leadership 3. Worship 4. Relevancy
5. Commitment 6. Excellence 7. Ministry 8. Christianity

TABLE OF
CONTENTS

DEDICATION

I lovingly dedicate this document to my family, the late, Leo H. Davis, Sr. where it all started, and whom I revere even in his absence. To my wonderful mother, Dorcas L. Davis, who even to this day will not allow a day to pass without covering me with prayer over the phone both morning and night. To my behind the scenes brother, Alvin G. Davis, you always give me the support when needed, and I love and appreciate you for that.

To the one of the greatest church choirs that I have ever had the privilege of serving with, the Blvd. Sanctuary Chorus. We have developed musically, spiritually and relationally as a unit to overcome some of the greatest obstacles. You were the constant that held together the congregation in the midst of tumultuous transitional experiences. It was the music that kept the people coming. It was the music that healed the hurting hearts. It was the music that yielded forth the fruit of lost souls for the kingdom. I've come to really understand how and why ministry functions because of each of you, past and present. For this, I give God praise.

Soli Deo Gloria

ENDORSEMENTS

"Dr. Leo Davis is not only gifted, but wise. An extraordinary church leader and a person of deep faith, Dr. Davis is articulate and generous in sharing wisdom acquired through his years of church experience and ministry. This book is full of insight—theologically sound and "road tested" through years of disciplined engagement with church congregations and leaders. Read this book and feel the inspiration of the Spirit move you to new levels of vitality, passion and transformation in your ministry! *–Rev. Cheryl Cornish Senior Pastor- First Congregational United Church of Christ. Memphis, TN.*

"One of the greatest joys and blessings of my forty plus years of pastoral ministry has been knowing and working with Dr. Leo H. Davis, Jr. And this book, NO GIMMICKS is a must read for every serious and committed person of faith. Far much more than a technical how-to manual of worship ministry, this book stands alone as a testimony of Dr. Davis's faith journey and his four decades of authentic, powerful, and relevant leadership in music and worship ministry. *– Reverend Dr. Alvin O'Neal Jackson, Senior Pastor Park Avenue Christian Church (Disciples of Christ) and United Church of Christ – New York, New York*

"Dr. Davis shares insights and experiences, from over 25 years in music ministry, in a conversational manner that will appeal to those contemplating, beginning or fully invested in ministry. He encourages the reader to see music ministry as a spiritual "journey" of excellence that begins with a "call," is filled with "passion" and "empowered... equipped...and endowed" by God. Dr. Davis gives advice that is sincere, practical, engaging, reflective and purposeful. Indeed, there are No Gimmicks in this book. It's the real deal! *– Dr. Rosephanye Powell-Charles W. Barkley Endowed Professor and Professor of Voice at Auburn University- Auburn, AL.*

"In a world of seemingly endless gospel entertainment and the relentless pursuit of cash, cameras, and crowds, it is refreshing to read a serious, sober, and spiritual look at worship ministry in the 21st century. A must read for all who want to be committed, excellent, and relevant." *– Dr. Frank A. Thomas. Nettie Sweeney and Hugh Th. Miller Professor of Homiletics/ Director of the Academy of Preaching and Celebration. Christian Theological Seminary, Indianapolis, IND.*

"In addition to being a great personal friend and mentor, I believe Dr. Leo Davis is a profound gift to all who are seeking to find their purpose, refine their gift, and answer the call God has placed on their lives. His book has reassured me of my personal journey as it has challenged and motivated me to examine what external and internal voices inform my vocation. This book has pushed me to believe in myself without question or pause, continue to strengthen my faith in God, and to live a passionate and purpose filled life by imparting practical spirituality to things that can get so "deep and religious" in the church. This book is for all who are seeking ministry over mediocrity as they pursue excellence and a purpose driven life!" *– Roland Jack, Safe Haven Management, CEO*

"In No Gimmicks, Dr. Leo Davis's four decades of successful leadership using his gifts, talents, academic training and experiences as a minister of music and worship shines through. He provides refreshing, candid, insightful, and practical directives for those entrusted with musical leadership in the church. In this instructive and accessible book, Dr. Davis juxtaposes the need for theological and cultural relevance, personal commitment, and musical excellence against a culture of anti-intellectualism, laxity, and self-centered musical leadership. This book will find a home in the libraries of pastors, music directors, musicians, and those who select and supervise them!"
– Dr. W. James Abbington, Associate Professor of Church Music and Worship, Candler School of Theology, Emory University, Atlanta, GA

"Dr. Davis has produced a robust scaffold for the construction of a sound life in Worship Ministry. Building upon proven principles, "No Gimmicks" provides the reader with the requisite tools for success at every stage. He steps up to the mic and amplifies standards of excellence, modeled over decades in practice, now in print for generations to come. Bravo!" *– Darin Atwater. Founder/Artistic Director at Soulful Symphony, Inc and Chairman & CEO @H2O Entertainment Group, LLC*

"No Gimmicks is an incisive text for every minister of worship and an invaluable resource to cultivate the dialogue between Pastors and those who serve in the ministry of music. Drawing upon almost 4 decades of excellence in ministry, Dr. Davis now offers a necessary perspective that will empower the body of Christ in the 21st century." *– Rev. J. Lawrence Turner, Senior Pastor- Mississippi Boulevard Christian Church (Disciples of Christ), Memphis, TN.*

"In every generation, there will emerge master teachers with the ability to capture the heart of a matter and communicate it in such a way, as to make it palatable to both small and great. Dr. Leo Davis is such an individual; and with this literary offering, will lift the reader to comprehend both the depths and the heights of life and the music ministry. You will be informed, challenged and blessed" – *Dr. Judith McAllister, President – International Music Department COGIC, Inc.*

"Dr. Davis' journal of 40 years in church music ministry is a must read for both "want-to be's" and "been there's." It is an invaluable manual of benchmarks for preparation and evaluation. His life's work confirms the necessity and value of finding and understanding one's purpose and commitment thereto - a model to be emulated. Indeed, Dr. Davis attests and affirms that there are NO GIMMICKS to excellence." – *Roland M. Carter, Professor Emeritus. University of Tn. at Chattanooga*

"Renowned Minister of Music, Dr. Leo H. Davis is the "Gold Standard" with an uncompromising commitment to excellence, spiritual and theological integrity. He is a great gift to the body of Christ and now his book, No Gimmicks, is a gift to Pastor and Minister of Music alike who aspire to command heaven's attention. – *Dr. Gina M. Stewart: Senior Pastor-Christ MB Church-Memphis*

CHAPTER 1
No Gimmicks: The Introduction

Whoever make a hit they the best (that's a gimmick)
You sell records based on how you dress (that's a gimmick)
Hey yo, that tongue-twistin ****, that's kinda fresh (that's a gimmick)
What's when you're soft but you're frontin like you're stressed?
(that's a gimmick)
What's when you're only into rap to get paid? (that's a gimmick)
What's when you're yellin and screamin up on stage?
(that's a gimmick)
When your career is numbered by days? (that's a gimmick)
What's when your lyrical style is just a faze? (that's a gimmick)
Lyric by LORD FINESSE

In December of 2013, immediately following the Mississippi Boulevard Christian Church's Annual Christmas Concert, our senior pastor, Rev. J. Lawrence Turner, expressed his interest in celebrating my 25 years of service to the church. Although I would have been deeply moved by a simple event—something like a special Sunday morning service followed by a reception in the fellowship hall—Pastor Turner's initial questions signaled his intent to host a much larger celebration. It was a celebration beyond my wildest dreams, an absolutely unbelievable weekend; certainly the highpoint of my twenty-five years of ministry at Mississippi Boulevard Christian Church. I cannot think of any other event that has been able to capture the artistry, audience engagement, and spirit that rested on the entire weekend celebration from Friday, July 18th through Sunday, July 20th. At the concert we were blessed to have performances rendered by the unique blend of the church community voices within the 150-voice Celebration of the Arts Chorus, along with a fine cadre of musical colleagues, dear friends, and surrogate family members, including (but not limited to):

▷ *Nathaniel Gumbs: Minister of Worship Arts /Organist at the Friendship Baptist Church, Charlotte, North Carolina. Doctoral Student, Organ Performance and Pedagogy, Eastman School of Music (University of Rochester), Rochester, New York*
▷ *Brandon Boyd: Minister of Music at the Bethel AME Church, Tallahassee, Florida. Doctoral Student -Choral Conducting (Florida State University), Tallahassee, Florida.*
▷ *Dr. W. James Abbington: Associate Professor of Church Music and Worship, Candler School of Theology (Emory University), Atlanta, GA.*
▷ *Dr. Roland Carter: Professor Emeritus, the University of Tennessee at Chattanooga. Founder and CEO of Mar-vel Publishing Company. Chattanooga, TN.*
▷ *Patrick Dailey: counter-tenor and recent graduate of Morgan State University and Boston University (Vocal Performance Major). Boston, MA.*
▷ *Paul Heflin: Renowned Tenor and Ordained Minister (Fredericksburg, VA.)*
▷ *Pastor Shirley Caesar: Iconic Gospel Artist. Multiple Grammy Award Nominee and 11 time winner. Senior Pastor of the Mt. Calvary Word of Faith Church, Raleigh, North Carolina*

▷ *Gaye Arbuckle: National Gospel Recording Artist. Serves as Minister of Music for Concord Church, Dallas, Texas*
▷ *Kathy Taylor: National Gospel Recording Artist Songwriter, Producer. Serves as the Minister of Music for the Windsor Village United Methodist Church, Houston, Texas*
▷ *V. Michael Mckay: Conductor, Clinician, song writer and author. Two Time Dove award winner and inductee into the Gospel Hall of Fame (2000). Houston, Texas*
▷ *Donald Lawrence: American Gospel Songwriter, record producer and artist. Stellar Award Winner for three consecutive years (2006-2008). Chicago, IL.*
▷ *Kurt Carr: American Gospel music composer and performer. Winner of four Stellar awards. Houston. Texas*
▷ *Ricky Dillard: American Gospel Recording Artist. Singer and Conductor. Chicago, IL.*

The next night, at the Black Tie Dinner, we were treated to performances by pianist, Gale Jones Murphy, noted soprano, Valetta Brinson, baritone, Laurence Albert, counter-tenor Patrick Dailey, and a battery of tributes from colleagues and several individuals that I have come to think of as my surrogate children. Many of them were afforded the opportunity to speak, perform, and roast me. Theirs were among the most moving tributes. I was so gratified by the young men and women whom God has allowed me to engage in healthy and supportive relationships. I was filled with joy as I thought about my journey and those who included me in their calling. On Sunday morning, we were treated to special musical performances from Nathaniel Gumbs and Gale Jones Murphy along with other friends Min. Avis Graves, Dr. Tony McNeil, and one of my dear surrogate sons, Mr. Karlos Nichols, of New York City, who all together, blended their worship with ours at our weekly worship celebration.

The entire weekend exemplified the musical excellence and diversity that I have sought to provide throughout my career in worship ministry. All of my life, I have aspired to blend gospel with the classical, the intellectual with the emotional, the economically empowered with the economically challenged—high church with low church. And not only were the iconic Contemporary Gospel artists in attendance and on the performance roster, but the concert included pieces like the opening organ prelude, J. S. Bach's Prelude and Fugue in D Major BWV. 532 , Cesar Franck, Psalm 150, to Dr. Nathan Carter's arrangement of "It Pays To Serve Jesus." All weekend long, we were able to experience the glory and majesty of our Lord and Savior Jesus Christ, featuring the best of the African American worship experience—spontaneous worship moments joined with the display of artistic prowess.

Once I received the vision from my pastor, I knew I would need some help planning this major event. So I called Mr. Larry Crawford. He was a God-send to say the least. Larry had successfully led two major tributes to legendary gospel icons, Mr. Kurt Carr, and Pastor Shirley Caesar. I knew of the magnitude of his work and connections, however I was somewhat hesitant about whether or not he would capture my heart and vision successfully.

My initial meeting brought an enormous level of peace to my spirit and confirmation per my decision to have Mr. Crawford collaborate with the church on this endeavor. Once the primary stakeholders met (i.e. Pastor Turner and Larry Crawford), I was convinced of the success of the event. Next was to select a core team to assist with all of the arduous planning over the next several months. In addition, we had to immediately find a date that would work best, and strategically ensure that no other major church and community event would collide with ours. Before I knew it, we were off and running...from the finalization of a full weekend of festivities, to the initial guest artist(s) performing, to my complete decision-making ability with regard to the program details—the event was slated and sanctioned by the Holy Spirit to be a sure success. With the overarching goal in mind, the weekend would feel like a journey that spoke widely to the musical diversity of the African American Church music experience. I knew that there had to be an added component of performers who were excellent in the field of church music performance, in addition to the cadre of top notch gospel artistry.

In addition to the performing artists, I began to sense that this weekend would encompass a larger chorus of participants who were not members of the chorus at the Blvd. I was initially torn about whether or not our members would feel somewhat overlooked if outsiders were involved. However my scope of performance and artistry had evolved as a result of my growth at the Blvd. Our collaborations with the Memphis Symphony Orchestra, Memphis City Public Schools, and other music and church organizations had warranted the expectation to open the chorus up to those individuals who had shared in my growth and success while here in the Memphis, TN., and WOW, did they come to share. Our chorus rehearsals were filled with numbers from 140 to 155 chorus members who gladly met for rehearsal twice per week for approximately five consecutive weeks of preparation. This chorus depicted individuals from choral directors, singers, professionals to the working class (which is the experience each Sunday at the Blvd.), and varied African American worship experiences throughout the continental USA.

This was one event that represented an entire life's journey; and I want this book to share that ministry journey with you. Great moments do not happen in a day. Wonderfully planned concerts don't happen overnight. In this book, I want to offer autobiographical nuggets related to specific issues in ministry, which will hopefully bring insight to you on how you might engage challenges, celebrate successes and avoid failures. In Chapter 2, I will succinctly discuss the start and the initiation of "the call" to worship ministry. *How does an individual clearly discern the right ministerial path for their lives? I have several gifts within and without of this field. What's my passion?* In chapter 3, I will begin to establish clarity about my own personal life, including the role models set before me from childhood and the sacrifices of my parents. The goal is to help you to think about your public calling within the context of your personal narrative. With that in mind, I will reminisce from my early path to my current status. In Chapter 4, I desire to formulate a clear chronological time-table of my historical and relational view of the relationships with each of the Pastoral Leads during my tenure at Mississippi Boulevard Christian. In addition, I will talk about the necessity of a healthy relationship between the Pastor and the Musician within the church. I will also introduce to you some of the wisest pastors and musicians I know, who will speak to the power struggle between worship leader and senior pastor. Chapter 5 will elaborate on the necessity of constructing a music philosophy that is rooted in church history and the pastor's vision. *What are the non-negotiables? Can we be friends, really? How much of my personal life should my staff be involved in? Why is worship planning important? In this chapter, we will look at a few recommendations from pastors and musicians from around the country, in terms of worship planning.* I will also share comments from pastors and musicians on worship, relationship, and communication. In Chapter 6, I will deal with administrative duties. *What are some simple things that will keep us organized on a consistent basis? How do I manage staff, plan and create budgets, and all of the other administrative duties, and still have time to be creative and continue developing my own personal skills? Can that really happen? Do I have to allow my personal skills to go lacking?* In this chapter, I will also discuss whether or not it is possible to achieve excellence on a weekly basis. *What does "excellence," look like? How is it shaped to create "excellence" from rehearsals to the "worship experience?"* In chapter 7, we will talk about ministry evolution and development. Is it important to have multiple choirs, and how does one keep the music ministry relevant despite an ever-evolving church culture?

Chapter 8 is a tough one. Why? Because at some point or another, we all will come into contact with difficult people, and we must learn how to deal with them accordingly. *What if the "difficult party" is me? How do I come to grips with some stark realities?* Conflict manifests the true attributes of who we really are. In order to manage conflict, then we must deal with and learn all of the lessons made available to build character. And finally, in Chapter 9, it is important that we know how to transition. There are several scenarios that will be presented to help us differentiate transitioning from your job to reinventing yourself beyond your job. The key is that we carefully hear all of the surrounding "voices around us, and move according to the will of God for our lives."

From my first experiences playing as a music ministry assistant to my father at the Greater Galilee Missionary Baptist Church, in Chicago, IL, through my simultaneous service at Chicago's Martin Temple AME Zion Church, and St. Luke Church of God in Christ, through my undergraduate studies, and the Charles Street AME Church, through graduate education in Boston, I can truly say that God has led me through the water, the flood, and the fire with the power of His blood. I offer this book and my journey as an example of what God can do with a life offered to him, and I hope that my experiences will offer wisdom to those at different points on their sojourn in worship ministry.

I know a lot of queries will surround my choice of the title, *NO GIMMICKS,* but I named it this for a reason. Our culture continues to shift from the value of consistency and hard labor to achieving quick GIMMICKS. There are shortcuts to everything, however it's the undergirding foundation of ethics that makes the outcome truly substantive. Fanny Crosby's lyrics, "this is my story, this is my song" helped me to frame this project. I have been privileged to spend most of my life engaged in helping others to sing their songs; and finally, I get to tell my story. No shortcuts. No gimmicks. Just me.

CHAPTER 2
Hearing the Call – Am I Leadership Material?

> "The uncalled life is an autonomous existence in which there is no intrusion, disruption, or redefinition, no appearance, or utterance of the Holy."
> – *Walter Brueggeman*

W hat does it mean to be called? How does one know that he or she is living out their calling? Most importantly, what are some necessary tools that every called person needs in order to maintain and sustain their calling? In this chapter, I want to tackle these questions in a conversational manner. I want to offer my personal observations, leadership failures, life lessons, and collaborative experiences in the hopes that you, too, will hear the call and obey it. But before we delve any further into this exciting journey together, let me debunk a common misnomer about one's calling.

It has been said that one's calling can exist in the absence of relationship with God. To this, I vehemently disagree. In my humble opinion, one's calling can *only* be experienced and enjoyed *after* the called one is in relationship with the One calling. In other words, our active calling is tied to our active relationship with Jesus Christ. Sure, we have nudges and passions. Most certainly, we have talents and gifts. But when we embrace our calling, we recognize there is something greater than my gift pulling me toward the God who has gifted me. This is when you step into your calling. You know you are called when you pay attention to mentors and teachers who do what you do, and you want to learn everything there is to know about that subject. You know you are called when you try to resist the pull to do it, and like Jeremiah, it becomes like "fire shut up in your bones." You can't resist it even when you try to ignore it. You can't deny it because everybody sees it on you. If they paid you for it, you would do it. If they didn't pay you for it, you would still do it. Because you are called—and when you are called, you have an assurance in God's investment in you that no person, place, or thing can take away. When you are called, you become sick and tired of mediocrity. Whether that is mediocrity from your department at church on a week-to-week basis, or mediocrity from your production team at work. When you are called, you move toward making productive and realistic changes. You recognize that you are called to make a difference and not settle. Personally, I know that I am called by God to make a difference and to not accept mediocrity. I am also called to proclaim, promote and prove that excellence in music ministry still prevails.

> BECAUSE YOU ARE CALLED—AND WHEN YOU ARE CALLED, YOU HAVE AN ASSURANCE IN GOD'S INVESTMENT IN YOU THAT NO PERSON, PLACE, OR THING CAN TAKE AWAY.

My dad, Leo H. Davis, Sr. was a fine musician, yet he had a great heart and love for diverse music in the black church. He was a six-foot tall, brownskinned, handsome black man who worked for the city highway patrol in Chicago. His initial quest was to become a medical doctor. Yet he had a deep passion for the music of the church. At the age of 10, he began serving as lead organist for the New Hope Baptist Church on Ball Road, in Memphis, TN, while studying with Mrs. Ruth Whalum, the organist for the Metropolitan Baptist Church on Walker Avenue, across from LeMoyne Owen Gardens, my father's place of residence in the late 1930's. As such, he was dedicated to preserving the music of black composers and sought to interpret the music of the choral masters while educating the congregation-at-large. As a young teenager, I can recall attending a music workshop with my father at the Monumental Baptist Church on the South Side of Chicago. Monumental Baptist Church (Hortense Love was the minister of music at that time) set the tone for great church music as well as other churches in the late 60's and early 70's, like Bethesda Baptist Church (Florence Stith – Minister of Music), and Martin Temple A.ME Zion Church (Dr. Charles Clency – Minister of Music). Mr. William Dawson was one of the original progenitors of the arranged concert spiritual for SATB voices, and one of the things I can recall from that workshop is how he communicated and interpreted music. I can still see him looking over his glasses at the chorus while singing his arrangement of "Ezekiel Saw

WHEN YOU ARE CALLED, YOU ALLOW THE TRACKS OF YESTERDAY TO GUIDE YOU, BUT YOU ALLOW THE VOICE OF GOD TO DEFINE YOU.

de Wheel," and shouting to the pianist, "I don't need you playing all of those notes. Just give me the Bb major chord, and we can go from there." He explained to the chorus how he wanted "wheel" to be interpreted via accents on the opening "doom a loom's," etc. Needless to say, to a young teenager, I was completely inundated by the entire experience. I enjoyed wonderful instrumentation and ingenious arrangements, both vocally and musically, and my dad exposed me to all of that.

So it was no surprise to my family that I decided to follow in my dad's footsteps. Many of us follow in the footsteps of our parents or guardians. That's guidance. But calling is something deeper. When you are called, you allow the tracks of yesterday to guide you, but you allow the voice of God to define you. As a musician, I could've chosen many different paths. I could've become a professor teaching at the doctoral level. I could've dedicated my life to duplicate the heart of my father's passions, but when God called me, he also defined me. He gave me a passion for the church in a way I can't explain. He gave me a love for His people that just won't go away. He gave me a heart for the house of the Lord that gives me contentment within my passion for music. My calling was realized when my passion and purpose collided.

In a similar manner, I believe the same will happen to you as you delve into a deeper relationship with Christ. When you become established in the faith and conversant with your Maker, He will give you the assurance and the approval necessary to execute his call. He will grant you favor to meet the right people at the right time, who will sharpen and strengthen your gift(s). He will give you the peace that surpasses understanding so you never feel inadequate when the temptation comes to compare yourself to someone else. This is the call of God. It is the unapologetic assurance that something greater in you is greater than you. This is the call of God—when your authenticity moves above and beyond your ability. This is the call of God. When you embrace that call, people will be inspired by your teaching, uplifted by your singing, encouraged by your playing, and transformed by your writing.

> WHEN YOU EMBRACE THAT CALL, PEOPLE WILL BE INSPIRED BY YOUR TEACHING, UPLIFTED BY YOUR SINGING, ENCOURAGED BY YOUR PLAYING, AND TRANSFORMED BY YOUR WRITING.

A few months ago, I read a quote on social media. I believe it is relevant for the subject of calling. The post read, "The mediocre teacher tells. The good teacher explains. The superior teacher demonstrates. The great teacher inspires." After I read these words, I added, "and the exceptional teacher exhibits all of the above." I don't know about you, but if I am going to do something for God, I want to be exceptional at it.

I want to embody the telling, the explaining, the demonstration and the inspiration all at the same time. I want people to be so inspired by the way I live out my calling, they will be challenged to live out their calling better every time they encounter me. If they meet me on Sunday as I am directing the service, I want them to be inspired when they encounter me functioning in my passion. If they read words from a book I've written, I want them to be inspired. Whatever I do with this passion for music and this calling to teach, I want God to be pleased and I want His people to be radically inspired to make a difference. How about you?

PASSION, FAITH AND CHARACTER

If someone were to ask you, *"What is your calling,"* how would you respond? I believe our calling is comprised of three basic tenets: personal passion, active faith, and a developed character. In the opening lines of this chapter you read Walter Brueggeman's quote, but allow me to repeat it here: "the uncalled life is an autonomous existence in which there is no intrusion, disruption, or redefinition, no appearance, or utterance of the holy." In other words, the uncalled life is a boring life. The uncalled life is a predictable life. The uncalled life is a man-centered, goal-oriented, monolithic experience. You will live, go to school, get married, have children, buy a home, sell the home, retire, get old, and die. This is what you can expect if you decide to travel down the road of no calling. But for those of us who want more out of life, we must be willing to travel down the road of calling. On this road, there are dead ends streets called "uncertainty." On this road, there is nervousness and trepidation. On this road, you won't be able to make every decision on your own. In order to successfully travel on this road, you will have to contact your Heavenly Father for GPS instructions. On this road, God Himself will speak boldly to you about your life and His divine appointment concerning you. This is why you must first learn and relearn how to manage your passions correctly. When you manage your passions, you will become clear about your assignment. When you are in tune with your passions, you will know when it's time to let go of one assignment and move on to the next one. Let's talk for a moment about the implications of passion.

After 26 years of music ministry leadership, I am serving under the fifth pastorate at Mississippi Boulevard. I love my church, and I love the community that God has called me to serve. At the same time, I cannot say that every day has been easy or fulfilling. Some days, I had to return back to the drawing board and ask God to "order my steps" in His word again and again. As a consistent barometer for self-examination, I have learned to ask myself on a weekly basis, "Are you functioning in your passion, Leo?" Then, I put systems in place to answer that question so that I don't allow the ephemerality of my fleeting emotions to dictate my decisions. I put a system in place that evaluates weekly outcomes and results. If I complete the work but it feels like drudgery, I take note of that because that can mean one of two things—*either I am working beyond my season or I am not functioning in my passion.* When you are called, God gives you the grace to passionately express your gifts. When you are called and graced but not placed, it could mean you need to seek God about relocating elsewhere. Why? Because you will always be frustrated when your gift does not bear fruit. You will always feel inadequate in soil that isn't nurturing your growth. When you have to become what someone else wants in order to do what you've been purposed to do, you are trying to fit your gift in a room too small for your calling. Take note of these moments

> YOU WILL ALWAYS BE FRUSTRATED WHEN YOUR GIFT DOES NOT BEAR FRUIT.

because it could mean you are working beyond your season of expiration or you are not functioning at the level of your calling. Learn from my mistakes— refuse to waste precious time and resources, creativity, and health working at the wrong assignment. When you are working in an arena that is not consistent with your calling, it's not service; it's slavery. You are out of place because you are out of passion. That's like being an employee at Ruth's Chris, but clocking in at McDonald's. You'll never see the reward of your labor because you're not in the right place. You're working but you are exhausted. You're excited for a little while, but the weight of responsibility becomes greater than the joy of opportunity. Take note of these things, because when your passion drops, purpose will soon retire. Where joy ceases to exist, commitment becomes hard to maintain. Don't waste your time feeding people and places who don't feed you. Instead, spend time with God and get clarity and direction about your passion.

I've met many people who, for years, functioned out of loyalty and not calling. In the end, it always damages you in ways you can't see. But when you allow God to guide your calling by the passion He deposited in you (and not by the people connected to you), you will always land on the perfect will of God for your life. If you ignore the promptings of God, you will become bitter and callous. Even worse, you will depend on people to tell you something about your life that only God can tell you. Take note when your spirit says, "Something isn't right." Learn to clearly delineate the still, small voice of God from the loud, verbose opinions of people. When you hear from God, you will experience success. When you change for people, you will experience distress.

Psalm 75:6-7 states, "No one from the east or the west or from the desert can exalt themselves. It is God who exalts: he brings one down, he exalts another." When you are in alignment with your calling, you will trust His ultimate plan for your life. You will live a life of faith, and not fear. You will live for purpose, and not popularity. You will also make sure that your passion is functioning at a high level of productivity. How does one do that exactly? I believe we begin that process by committing to live a life of overflow. By this I mean, we commit to daily fellowship with God. This helps us to reconcile the commitment of our call with the God who called us. It is not easy, but when you commit to it, it will be worthwhile.

Practically speaking, my faith is the most important component of my calling. If I am always working, working, working, and not resting, I will not be able to serve at the greatest level of purpose and passion. This means I must intentionally regulate my schedule in such a way that I insert breaks when needed. Especially after major events, I try to set up a nice getaway of some sort, or create something worth looking forward to. This drives my faith and reinvigorates my passion because small rewards help me to remain motivated. It is just as important to plan for fun as much as you plan for work. Your passion must have some time to recharge. Your life can't experience the best if you aren't getting sufficient rest. Therefore, resist the tendency to think that the church, the organization, or the team can't go on without you. One of the greatest hindrances to a successful, vibrant, and passionate life is our own damaged self-perception. If no one has told you this before, allow me to clarify something for you: you have full control of how you live your life. You have full control of how many days people can have access to you. You have the power to pause and allow God to refill and refuel you.

The problem is, we don't always assume that power. Instead, we give it away to people who don't value what God has deposited inside of us. This is unhealthy and unwise. Don't allow the demands of your call to get in the way of your joy. Don't allow people to control your entire life. If you let work overwork you, it will. If you let people take advantage of you, they will. If they know you will work harder for less, they will give you less and expect more. But if you live out of the overflow, you will discover righteousness, peace, and joy in the Holy Ghost.

The overflow is for others. The cup is for you. When your faith is fueled by passion, God will satisfy your needs. When your faith is fueled by passion, you will have enough to give to others out of your excess, not your essentials. If you set intentional time in your day to meditate on the Lord and pray, you won't be frustrated with emails and phone calls. Instead, you will designate time to respond to them, while you make it a priority to speak to *Him*. This is one way to keep your passion level high. Another way to maintain passion through faith is to ask yourself some essential questions on a daily, weekly, or monthly basis:

1. Am I worshipping and praying with passion?
2. Am I passionate about God's word?
3. How can I receive grace in spite of my failures?
4. What do I possess to work with my passion?
5. Do I rest with passion?
6. Whose voice do I listen for?
7. Are passionate people around me?
8. What does pleasing God look like?

Allow me to briefly expound on each of these questions, and the rationale behind them. Merriam Webster defines passion as, "a strong feeling of enthusiasm or excitement for something." Personally, my passion is three-fold. I am passionate about music. I am passionate about developing and executing music that is diverse and relevant; and I desire to execute it with excellence. I am passionate about mentoring young musicians in order to prepare the church for its future. Before you answer the above questions for yourself, first define your passion. Is your passion two-fold or three-fold? Are you passionate about one thing generally, and other things specifically? If so, write them down. Explore the reach of your passion, and be clear about what you care about. Second, answer the questions from that perspective of passion.

When I ask myself if I am worshipping and praying with passion, what I am really asking is, "When I pray, am I interweaving my passion for music, leadership, and mentorship into my prayer and devotional time?" I am not just asking about prayer in general; I am asking myself if I am praying with specificity and focus. There is no way to pray with passion if I am not spending quality time with God on a daily basis. And this deficiency (the lack of prayer) has been the root cause of failure in music ministry.

I can't speak for others, but I value highly my time with the Lord. For me, it is a non-negotiable. I have also had a prayer partner for over six years. I put personal Bible Study markers in place, and prayer time with God throughout my day to make sure I am serving from an overflow of passion. This correlates with being passionate about His Word. It is impossible to pray or worship effectively if I do not fully understand God's expectations vis-à-vis his Word. Examples of what God wants and expects are found in His word. Freedom from guilt and shame are also found in His word. Accepting God's grace doesn't happen organically. It happens because I read it and ingest it through and by His word.

I hope you now see why passion and faith must intersect consistently if you are going to live a life of calling. When God calls you, He builds you from the inside out. He cares about more than your gift; He cares about your heart. He cares GOD CARES ABOUT THE about your wholeness. He cares about your DEVELOPMENT OF YOUR FAITH, NOT JUST THE soul. When people call you for their own BRILLIANCE OF YOUR GIFT. purposes, they will promote you or demote you based on what you do. God, however, cares about who you are. God cares about the development of your faith, not just the brilliance of your gift. This is why I believe faith coincides with calling in an inextricable way.

When you walk in faith, you're walking in your calling. When you walk in faith, you are trusting in a God you can't see to lead you through the valley of the shadow of death. You are trusting in a God you can't always hear audibly to speak to you through a still, small voice and give you direction and interpretation. Faith is the unwavering assurance in God that He is faithful to keep his promises even when others let you down. Faith is the substance of things hoped for, and the evidence of things not seen. Without faith, it's impossible to please God. In the same way, if there is no faith, there can be no calling or passion. Faith helps you to believe when nothing around you says, "this is possible." Faith urges you to keep moving when the budget won't allow your dream to happen. Faith will introduce you to visionary leaders who can put language to your sound, words to your song, and choreography to your melody until you see in earth what God has spoken to you from heaven. When you walk in faith, you have confidence that others don't have.

You have assurance that only God can give. You have the ability to do through God's strength what you can't do through your gift alone.

How is faith developed? How is passion maintained? The answer to these questions can be summarized in one word: character. In order for faith to have longlasting presence and power in your life, and in order for passion to outlive the moment of a temporary experience or an event, you need to develop your character in God. If not, your calling will take you to a platform that your character can't keep you, if you fail to build it. Dr. Frank Anthony Thomas, who serves as the Nettie Sweeney and Hugh Th. Miller Professor of Homiletics and Director of The Academy of Preaching and Celebration at the Christian Theological Seminary (Indianapolis, Indiana), sites in *The Choice: Living Your Passion from the Inside Out:*

> "When you move from being a victim and live inside out, you're making daily progress in the new life that God has given you. When you live life inside out, your trust in God is stronger. Our convictions about the gospel are deeper. Our wisdom in knowing ourselves and our ability to overcome the troubles of the world is more profound. Our resistance to sin is more determined."

In essence, it is the cultivation of spiritual things that necessitates the growth of the natural things. Character, therefore, is built on the foundation of faith and passion. This may be why the Apostle John shares emphatically, "Beloved, I pray that you may prosper in all things and be in health, just as your soul prospers." Not only should we prosper in the areas that people can see, but we should also prosper in the areas that others cannot see. This is what Dr. Thomas prescribes in his publication, and these three principles, if taken seriously, will help to build character in the called. Dr. Thomas says:

1. Develop your character first, and then raise your gifts to the level of your character.

Many of us involved in the field of worship and creative arts spend a great deal of time developing our gift. Then, as an afterthought, we think about character. But in this day and time, we need to begin the other way around. Even though the world will tell you to craft your gift at a young age in order to be in the running's for success, Jesus would say that the essence of your character will give you power and latitude in areas that talent cannot sustain. Many times, we want to develop our gifts and then work on our character later. But God wants us to start from the "inside out." We want the "outside in" because it seems easier and more productive. Dr. Thomas agrees with the manner in which Jesus trained his disciples. Thomas writes, "Some of us are more concerned about our gifts and the exposure of our gifts rather than our character. But, if you're not careful, your gifts will take you beyond what your character can handle and when your gifts take you beyond your character, you end up in moral fault and trouble." Thank God we serve a gracious God who will not place us on certain platforms until He develops our character. Thank God He loves us that much, that He gives us choices and options. The primary reason we fail in the area of character is because we have not seen godliness and giftedness modeled in our lives. In my most recent years, there are several young men and some young women, with whom I have developed a surrogate parent relationship. They are extremely talented. However, God has placed them in my life to model true character before them. I am not flawless, but I am clear about who I am in Christ. I am vulnerable and honest with them and I continue to revisit my call and passion with them. Who do you have in your life to build character with?

2. The Gospel frees you from what people think of you, but more importantly, it frees you from what you think of yourself:

When you get free from what you think of yourself, it doesn't matter what other people think about you. If you feel worthless, devalued, and condemned by your past, guess what? Others will value you the way you value yourself. If you feel and think of yourself in demeaning ways, people and life will treat you as such. You must realize without a shadow of doubt, that "I've been redeemed from the curse of the law. I am the righteousness of God by faith in His son Christ Jesus;" and because, "I am fearfully and wonderfully made," God has uniquely formed me for a significant purpose. When you develop this part of your character, you won't allow people to change your God-given position in the earth. You will walk into the room confident, not cocky. You will embrace your position with humility, honor, and boldness. You will serve God with excellence because you won't enter from the posture of a slave. You will know that God calls you friend, and you will live from that biblical truth. This is all

> IT'S NOT ENOUGH TO HAVE FAITH IF YOU HAVE BEEN CONVINCED THAT THE GOD IN WHOM YOU BELIEVE, DOES NOT BELIEVE IN YOU.

character building. It's not enough to have faith if you have been convinced that the God in whom you believe, does not believe in you. It's not enough to have passion if you assume that God will punish you for making a mistake. You must walk in the victory of Christ's finished work on the cross. Because He died, you can live. His grace is sufficient, and you are more than a conqueror. Accepting this as truth, both biblically and experientially, will allow you to walk in favor with God and mankind.

3. Every situation is an opportunity:

Regardless of what happens to you in life, you can take it, mold it, and shape it into an opportunity. The question you must ask though, despite the circumstance, situation, or tragedy is this: "where is the opportunity here?" This kind of perspective only comes when we are in relationship with Jesus Christ. This kind of perspective will only become a part of you when you believe and accept that God's plans for you, are ultimately good. Knowing this will empower and encourage you to see every situation, both positive and negative, for your benefit. That means, every rehearsal—even the bad ones, will be used for your benefit. Every worship planning meeting—even the boring ones, will be used for your benefit. Every worship service can help you to embrace the next chapter of your life. That means, even the failures, are for my good. Even the delays, are for my good. This characterbuilder is not an easy declaration to embrace and embody. But with time, you will find yourself more composed and more clear when you accept God's word as true. Even me, I am still learning how to conquer negative self-talk. But the moment I feel those thoughts rise to the surface of my mind, I declare out loud, "I am more than a conqueror. I am fearfully and wonderfully made. The Lord has plans for my life and they are good and peaceful." As God builds character in you, you've got to learn to become your own calling coach. Nobody should speak into your life more than you. You are gifted. You are anointed. You are God's prized possession. And when he made you, God was showing off!

GET FREE FROM FEAR

Embracing these areas of character development will help us to surrender to what we've been called to do. The sooner we surrender in faith, the sooner we will be delivered from fear; and fear is nothing more than FALSE EVIDENCE APPEARING REAL. In my opinion, there are three areas of fear that must be conquered if we are going to move from calling into ministry leadership. First, we must be delivered from people's assumptions. Why? Because for too long, we have allowed people's knowledge of our past to imprison our future. If you allow people to control you by what they think they know about you, then you will never completely move into alignment with what God has for your life. You need to shift into your present and accept the fact that your past is just that—your past!

Secondly, we must be free from the assumption that we are not talented enough or skilled enough for the opportunities placed before us. Sure, someone is more gifted than you. Sure, someone can perform better than you. But you cannot be gripped by the fear of comparison. Instead, you've got to recognize that before the foundations of the world, God had already given you an earthly assignment according to the abilities distributed from heaven. Many times, due to past failures, experiences from childhood, demeaning verbal connotations, and insecurities, we accept negative self-talk and allow it to marinate in our minds and into our very lives. Some of us have been severely damaged, but that still is no excuse. You are more than capable to do this. You are more than competent to manage this. You are already equipped for your own designed assignment.

> YOU MAY NOT BE PERFECT (NOBODY IS), BUT YOU ARE PERFECTLY GIFTED FOR WHAT GOD PURPOSED YOU FOR.

You may not be perfect (nobody is), but you are perfectly gifted for what God purposed you for. Stop comparing yourself to others, and stop getting angry over what you didn't get. Focus on your journey and enjoy the ride! There are so many missed opportunities I've experienced because I allowed the fear of comparison to block my path. It was not until I recognized that God had empowered me, equipped me, and endowed me to do "immeasurably more than I could ever ask or think," that I was able to move forward accordingly.

Thirdly, in order to fully embrace your calling with passion, faith and character, you've got to stop fearing the platform, and instead, prepare your gift in private so God can use you in public. Spiritually, this means you must maintain an active and vibrant relationship with Jesus Christ. Surround yourself with sound doctrine, not opinionated subjectivity. Seek the One who gives creativity when you hit a wall. Take God at His word, and remind him of His promises in prayer. He promised to lead us into all truth. He promised to bring things back to our remembrance. He promised to complete what He began. These are the spiritual exercises you need to embrace every day.

Emotionally, we must be honest with ourselves about the constant battle we encounter with our inner feelings. When we are afraid, we must admit it. When we are uncomfortable, we must confess it. The more you come to grips with your emotions, the more likely you will be able to control them. But if you let your emotions rule you, they will.

Academically, we must resist the impulse to "go it alone," Instead, we must embrace training from an educational perspective. Don't be afraid of the academy. It's there to sharpen you. It's there to expose you. Everyone is not called to the academy. But for those of us who are, allow it to enhance your gift. Allow the knowledge you attain to intersect with the anointing God has given you. Watch God get the glory out of a gift that has been shaped by the fire of education. In my life, I have seen how the gift of education can help in so many ways. I am grateful for the opportunity that the academy has afforded me, and how God has brilliantly allowed me to combine the fruits of my training with the power of his anointing. I have seen diverse communities blessed, challenged, stretched and inspired by my exposure to different musical styles and training practices. This has encouraged me to live continually from the posture of a student. I am always willing to be corrected, exposed, and introduced to new terminologies, pedagogies, and systems because of my academic experiences.

Physically, you must take your health seriously. This means, you have to make a decision to raise the bar significantly—with what you eat, with how often you exercise, with dieting and resting accordingly. Now, I am no Mr. Atlas, but I am intentional about remaining physically fit. Rest is my top priority, and I try my best to minimize my stress levels. Stressful "drama" filled people are not apart of my daily connection, or conversation. I refuse to be filled with gossipy conversations and for the most part, I surround myself with like-minded individuals, who push me to succeed.

LIVING IN RHYTHM

When you enhance your life physically, academically, spiritually, and emotionally, then you are ready for ministry leadership. You are ready to live out your calling because you have committed to a life in rhythm. What do I mean by a life in rhythm? I'm so glad you asked. One of the most transformative books I have ever read was a book by Bruce B. Miller titled Your Life In Rhythm. When I read it, I fully engaged my time and efforts into this gem and I received such clarity and correction in my definition of balance and rhythm. I want to use the end of this chapter to recap some of the lessons learned from this masterful book.

We are often told to abdicate our bad habits and trends by finding balance. But Miller strongly opposes the phrase "balance, " and calmly suggests that we find our individualized "life rhythm." All around us, we experience life's rhythms. Nature has a rhythm. Our body functions in rhythm, and the world revolves around rhythm. I used to pressure myself into putting everything in my life on the scale of balance. But, no matter how hard I tried to do that, the scale would tilt because balance cannot be sustained over time (with a life filled with multiple projects to complete). I now see that the more I tap into my spiritual and personal rhythms, the more I am able to peacefully move into purpose without stress. Miller has created 10 essential rules for rhythm, and I will list them below as you think about your calling, your character, and your faith. If the rules help you, I encourage you to purchase his book as an additional resource. I believe it will help us all to become better ministry leaders generally, and better disciples of Jesus Christ specifically.

1. Get off the balance beam

2. Appreciate life's natural rhythms

3. Create a life mission statement

4. Live in sync with your current life stage

5. Release unrealistic expectations and comparisons

6. Seize opportunities

7. Anticipate what's next

8. Pace Yourself

9. Build life-enhancing rituals

10. Keep eternity in view

QUESTIONS FOR INTROSPECTION/ SMALL GROUP DISCUSSION

❶ What does it mean to be "called?"

❷ When did you first experience being "called?"

❸ How does an individual "manage his/her passions" in order to clarify their assignment?

❹ Is it possible to hold onto an assignment for too long? How can one tell the difference between a season you should press through and a sign that you should move on?

❺ What kind of results are you getting in your ministry? Are people being educated, challenged, and encouraged, or are they being stifled and bored? What do the results you are getting imply about your methods?

CHAPTER 3
Longevity – The Journey Begins

In the last chapter, we discussed the importance of knowing your calling. In this chapter, I want to encourage you to think about your public calling within the context of your personal narrative. Who are you? How did you get to where you are right now? Which parts of your history have most influenced your destiny? Where are you going and why are you headed in that direction? It is my firm belief that in order to have longevity in anything, you must embrace the journey in everything. It is when we "look back over our lives, and think things over," that we can truly see from whence we have come, and use that information as motivation to keep moving forward.

> IT IS GOD'S LOVE THAT CALLS THE UNQUALIFIED AND ANOINTS THE DISQUALIFIED. IT IS GOD'S LOVE THAT TURNS PERSONAL FAILURES INTO PUBLIC LESSONS.

Many times, over the last 40+ years, I have been challenged to think about God's call on my life. It has been amazing to find both music and faith interwoven into the fabric of every season of my existence. As you will soon discover, my journey is similar to many and at the same time, uniquely different from most. But in order for me to walk in my calling, I had to accept that God had called me to do something great. This was challenging to admit and difficult to acknowledge. Nevertheless, over time, I found God's redeeming love to be the most rewarding factor in my life. It is God's love that calls the unqualified and anoints the disqualified. It is God's love that turns personal failures into public lessons. Once you embrace God's unfailing love for you, and the blessing of God on you, then you will be in a better position to surrender to the call.

THE JOURNEY

My journey has been haunting yet exhilarating, daunting yet refreshing, splattered with mistakes yet governed by grace. As the songwriter testified, "I've had some good days, and I've had some hills to climb... but through it all, I won't complain because God has been good to me!" This is my journey. My father was an astutely peculiar gentleman who had a true affinity for Black Sacred Music. He always wanted to be found stretching himself and others toward the very best. He was born on August 14, 1929, in Memphis, Tennessee to the late John Henry Davis, a car union porter and Annie M. Jones, an entrepreneur with her brother, A. B. Jones. My grandfather was a devout deacon and choir member at the New Hope Baptist Church, of Memphis, TN. His middle child, Leo H. Davis, Sr., began serving as an organist at the age of ten. Leo's feet could barely touch the pedal board, but he had a keen ear and agile fingering that could approach any repertoire with ease.

While my father's talents were growing, he began to inquire about additional studies to enhance his craft. His first music teacher was Mrs. Ruth Whalum, an organist at the Metropolitan Baptist Church. It was usually a family outing for his parents and two siblings to walk across the street from their home at LeMoyne Gardens Public Housing to the church for his private lessons with Mrs. Whalum. My grandmother often spoke of how soft-spoken yet stern Mrs. Whalum was. She held my father accountable to all assignments and complimented him consistently for successful completion.

Everything was going very well for my family, and then, the unexpected happened. My grandfather, John Henry Davis, had an asthma attack in front of his three children and young wife. As a result, he died. He was 42 years old. My family became paralyzed. John's sudden death shocked the neighborhood. My grandmother was immediately summoned to the forefront of parental leadership, and had to lean on the support of brothers, sisters, aunts, and uncles, to assist with her three young teenage children. During this transition, the only girl, Addie, decided to visit the Pentecostal church not too far from their personal residence. That visit turned into a life-changing moment for she, her baby brother and mother. Within weeks, all had removed themselves from the doctrinal beliefs of the Baptist Church, and were newly dedicated members of the Temple Church of God In Christ, where the founder, Bishop Charles Harrison Mason served as Senior Pastor. I vividly recall my grandmother talking about my father's displeasure with their decision to leave New Hope Baptist Church for this new "worship" experience. But, the spontaneous worship style greatly enhanced his musical prowess.

Soon enough, the Davis residence became the primary lodging quarters for all guest speakers who visited the Temple Church of God in Christ. My grandmother was committed to the church, but that sometimes put the family into compromising situations. One morning, for example, my grandmother got up to iron an evangelist's robe in preparation for service later that night. My father awakened to not having his white shirt prepared as expected for school. He was so outraged, he completely overturned the ironing board and ripped the evangelist's robe to shreds. Of course, severe punishment followed. But this imbalanced loyalty to the church created resentment within my father. He carried this disdain against the Pentecostal Church for many years.

In the mid to late 1940's following my grandfather's death, several family members migrated north to Chicago. My great-uncle owned a dry cleaning business, and insisted that my grandmother make the transition north. Unbeknownst to her, this "call" for a new way of life would expose all three children to the social ills of the church. Annie Jones Davis would soon meet a handsome, tall, well-equipped young pastor, Elder Major Beverly, Sr., on the west side of Chicago (all of my grandmother's children became successful graduates of the John Marshall High School on the west side of Chicago). Both brothers enlisted into the Armed Services (Army), and returned to the Chicago area. The sister, Addie Lou Davis, pursued a college degree in education while the brothers returned home to marry beautiful women.

My father was interested in the medical program at John Marshall High School. But several years later, my grandmother married Elder Beverly and became a young pastor's wife in the Pentecostal church. This decision exposed my father to music and church on an entirely different level. Because my grandmother married a pastor, my father was introduced to thirty years of music ministry that would eventually engraft in me the same love for music that he had. It was this defining moment that served as a personal turning point for me, and a calling conduit for excellence and music in the church.

My father's love for music was evident by all who came to know him. He served as the Director of Music/Organist for the Greater Galilee Missionary Baptist Church under Rev. A.D. Strong from 1959-1979. My first job was serving under my dad as an organist in 1974 during my sophomore year of high school. My dad was earning $75.00/week, and he would pay me $35.00/week. The church did not pay me, but my father was determined to teach me how to value my gift by ensuring I was compensated. I still remember the first Sunday I received payment. He said: "This is why I am paying for you to study music. You will never allow anyone to take advantage of your gift." I thank God for those valuable lessons and sacrifices from both my father and mother.

During those pivotal years of development, I advanced in my musical studies at the Chicago Conservatory of Music. I also became acquainted with the musical genius of Dr. Cleveland Charles Clency and the Voices of Melody. I can still remember the first time I heard Dr. Clency and his semi-professional all black chorus. It was the second Sunday afternoon in July of 1974. I had never before heard such diversity in musical repertoire. I was completely enamored by the experience. Not long after that, Dr. Clency became my first organ professor and choral instructor. I tried to mimic everything he played. I memorized how he conducted his rehearsals. He embodied musical excellence in a way I had never seen before. This was my first exposure to music ministry excellence, but it wasn't my last.

Throughout my high school career, I excelled in my musical studies as first chair clarinet in the concert band; and at the age of 19, I took over my dad's position as Director of Music for the Greater Galilee Baptist Church. What a memorable experience. I learned so much at Greater Galilee. Most importantly, I learned how to be sensitive to God's voice. I had to hear from God about the music for the church, and I had to hear from God about the people I was called to serve. At Greater Galilee, I learned how to build relationships despite the hurdles. Certainly, I was young. Many of the volunteers were twice my age. But I learned to navigate through these troubling waters. I can vividly recall my first church choral concert at age 19. The program included: "The Battle Hymn of the Republic" by Peter Wilhousky, "I've been Buked" arranged by Hall Johnson, and several other gospel favorites. At an early age, I decided that every program would display a repertoire that was sacred and diverse.

As an Organ Performance major at Roosevelt University, I felt that I could be further challenged at Indiana University (Bloomington) School of Music. So I secretly applied to I.U. Bloomington, saved up for airfare, and prepared the audition repertoire. I met with the chair of the organ department, Dr. Oswald Ragatz, and successfully passed my audition. I.U. Bloomington was the place that fueled my love for the choral music tradition. I joined two choral ensembles: The Singing Hoosiers and the Doctoral Conducting Chorus; the latter of the two experienced top guest choral conductors every week! These guests would drill the doctoral students and scare them to the point of no return. But I didn't mind it at all. I viewed it as a free choral lesson, and I would mimic and research the information shared in class.

> I HAD BEEN WORKING IN CHURCH, AND CREATING FOR THE CHURCH, BUT WHAT WAS MISSING WAS THAT I HAD TO EXPERIENCE BEING THE CHURCH.

In December of 1979, while at I.U. Bloomington, I received Jesus Christ as my Lord and Savior. I was serving as the Director of Music for the Second Baptist Church in Bloomington, under Rev. E.D. Butler; and while there, many wonderful relationships were forged. One relationship, for which I will forever be grateful, is my dear friend, Dr. Peter Wherry. He took it upon himself to ask me if I had ever received Jesus Christ as my Lord and Savior. I told him no. Because of my upbringing, I viewed Christianity as "dos and don'ts," but Wherry taught me about receiving the love of God in my life. He brought the gospel to me in such a way that I was forever changed. I had been working in church, and creating for the church, but what was missing was that I had to experience *being* the church. That moment started my connection with Christ, and forced me to journey from within. I began to experience and exemplify his love in every area of my life.

Upon my father's illness in 1979, I made the decision to go back home and finish at Roosevelt University (Chicago). While at Roosevelt, I served two churches: Martin Temple A.M.E. Zion Church and the St. Luke Church of God in Christ. These were both wonderful experiences that exposed me to fresh music and solid ministry.

My call to music ministry continued during my college tenure in St. Louis, MO., with the New Sunny Mount Baptist Church (Chancel Choir). This was one of the finest choirs I inherited from a distant cousin, Mr. Ronald P. Metcalf. Ronald was a brilliant arranger, composer, pianist and choral director. That experience caused me to focus on developing my choral arrangement skills. The Chancel Choir at New Sunny Mount was a young adult choir of about 40-50 singers that could literally sing anything. What was so unique about the Chancel choir was their sensitivity to learn and execute music with precision and power. Ronald held them to a rigorous schedule of two rehearsals per week, which is currently a standard I have maintained up until this very moment.

Following my tenure in St. Louis, I pursued graduate studies at the University of Massachusetts (Lowell), and served as the Minister of Music for the Charles Street A.M.E. Church (Boston). Charles Street was a place of wonderful relationships and I learned, from Charles Street, the importance of pastoral care within the music ministry. I supervised mature adults at this church, but there was a unique bond shared between us. They were not the best singers, but I received such love and accountability from them. At Charles Street, we focused on not just singing but also on building personal relationships and community. It was from Boston MA., that I received the call in June, 1989 from Rev.

Alvin O. Jackson about the position of Minister of Music at Mississippi Boulevard Christian Church (Disciples of Christ). My tenure at the Blvd. has afforded me the opportunity for growth and development. I have learned how to develop and sustain relationships, and most importantly, I have matured in my walk

THE MORE COGNIZANT YOU ARE OF GOD'S CALL, THE MORE CONFIDENT YOU BECOME AT EXECUTING THAT CALL. NO CLARITY; NO CONFIDENCE.

with God. Now that I have taken each experience as a lesson to further understand my call, I am now able to:

☐Understand the difference between doing ministry and having a job

☐Realize what is being done with the "CALL" I've been assigned

☐Examine the fear that kept me from fully surrendering to the call

☐Ensure that all parties are maximizing their God-given potential

BE FULLY COGNIZANT OF GOD'S CALL

"The Lord gave me this message: "I knew you before I formed you in your mother's womb. Before you were born I set you apart and appointed you as my prophet to the nations." " O Sovereign Lord," I said, "I can't speak for you! I'm too young!" The Lord replied, "Don't say, 'I'm too young,' for you must go wherever I send you and say whatever I tell you. And don't be afraid of the people for I will be with you and will protect you. I, the Lord, have spoken!" Jeremiah 1:4-8

From the brief synopsis of my journey, I'm sure you can see that many times, I had to revisit the call at each stage or with each new assignment given. Even within the last few years, I had to look deep within myself as seasons changed, to get clarity about the call. The more cognizant you are of God's call, the more confident you become at executing that call. No clarity; no confidence. Jeremiah was called at a young age to do what hadn't been done. In the same way, you may be called by God to do what you haven't seen others do. But if you look at your history, you will see your destiny. You will see that all along, God was shaping you for this, equipping you for this, sharpening you for this, and preparing you for this.

Understand the difference between doing Ministry and having a job:

Effective music ministers understand their call to music ministry and are aware of the vocational implications that this call has for their life. The guiding premise is the "call from God." Your music lives as a result of the call, not the other way around. Frederick Buchener says, "The place God calls you to is where your deep gladness and the world's deep hunger meet." In essence, the calling is a combination of deep satisfaction and joy that you will receive when you use your God-given abilities to accomplish your assignment. It is a place that you know you could not exist without. Why? Because it's God given and God-directed!!! Many times, artists, musicians, and singers complicate matters with our own ideologies of success. We think life is about making money. But for me, life is about making an impact. When I do ministry, I am focused on making an impact. When I merely work at a job, I am only concerned about making money. Do you recognize the difference in your life?

> FREDERICK BUCHENER SAYS, "THE PLACE GOD CALLS YOU TO IS WHERE YOUR DEEP GLADNESS AND THE WORLD'S DEEP HUNGER MEET."

I believe we must revisit the process of our "call" to annihilate any confusion about doing ministry versus having a job. Thom S. Rainer and Eric Geiger look carefully at four values in their text, *Simple Church,* that help churches clearly appropriate guidelines for building disciples. I believe these values will help you to discern the differences for you as well:

#1. CLARITY

"That the God of our lord Jesus Christ, the Father of glory, may give unto you the spirit of wisdom and revelation in the knowledge of him: The eyes of your understanding being enlightened ; that ye may know what is the hope of His calling, and what the riches of the glory of His inheritance in the saints. " Ephesians 1:17-18

Clarity is the state or quality of being clear. As mentioned earlier, we gain clarity by spending quality time in His presence. When you are clear, you communicate clearly to others. When you are not clear, people find you hard to understand, difficult to follow, and complicated. If you are ministry-oriented, your language will tell on you. What you say about what you do and why you do it will speak volumes. If you are money-oriented, then as soon as a shift is made financially, you will be quick to look for a higher-paying alternative, even if that alternative is spiritually deficient. In what areas do you need more clarity? How long have you sought the Lord about your questions and concerns? The answer is sometimes in the questions you ask, and not the response you receive.

#2. MOVEMENT:

"But one thing I do: forgetting what lies behind and staining forward to what lies ahead, I press on toward the goal for the prize of the upward call of god in Christ Jesus." Philippians 3:14

Movement is what causes a person to go to the next step, or into greater areas of commitment. In order to embrace our narrative, we must be willing to move forward and not backward. Non-movement is not motion. If you are stuck, you are just as unclear as the person moving backward. An individual who has no commitment to ministry, but is only producing according to their job description, will function as such with no vision and no movement. The goal is forward movement. How are you making forward moves to accomplish God's call in your life? What setbacks have you experienced, and how have you planned to bounce back from them?

#3. ALIGNMENT:

"For I do not understand my own actions. For I do not do what I want, but I do the very thing I hate." Romans. 7:15

"Watch and pray that you may not enter into temptation. The spirit indeed is willing, but the flesh is weak." St. Mark 14:38

To align oneself to anything, you must put yourself in a straight line or bring yourself into parallel syncopation with the thing you are aligning yourself to. It is impossible to embrace God's call if your heart is not aligned with God's will. Certainly, we will have seasons of temptation. Sure, we will make mistakes. We are in a perpetual war between the will of our flesh and the will of God. But at some point, your spirit will crave alignment when you are truly living according to God's will. If you are money-minded, you will ask "what's in it for me." If you are mission-minded, you will ask God to "remove me from the equation. Let them see more of you and less of me." *What is in it for Me?* That's an essential question that we all ask as we revisit our call. It is not just enough to be obedient to God; we also have to do His will with the right attitude. The Word of God tells us that God not only looks at our actions; He also looks at the motives behind our actions. So, even though we do exactly what God tells us to do, it will not matter if we do not do it with the right attitude. (Jeremiah 17:10).

IF YOU ARE MONEY-MINDED, YOU WILL ASK "WHAT'S IN IT FOR ME." IF YOU ARE MISSION-MINDED, YOU WILL ASK GOD TO "REMOVE ME FROM THE EQUATION. LET THEM SEE MORE OF YOU AND LESS OF ME."

What do I Need to Do to Get My Heart in Alignment? There are moments that human frailty will kick in as a result of life experiences. However, our humanness does not negate our call to do the right thing. With that in mind, it is not enough to solely do what God wants us to do. We also must have the right attitude when we do it. If we have done the right thing but with the wrong attitude, we need to quickly repent to God about it. The great thing about God is that He will forgive us just as quickly as we apologize. God does not stop loving us even when we mess up. But it is our job to acknowledge Him in all of our ways, and pray that God will help us to get our hearts in alignment with His will.

#4. FOCUS:

Focus is the commitment to abandon everything that falls outside of your desired goal. Focus requires saying "yes" to the best, and "no" to everything else. Focus is the element that gives power and energy to clarity, movement, and alignment. Thus, as we consider the "call", it is imperative that we ask ourselves some important questions. It is also important that we take the time to chart our own journey. What led you to this point? How did you get here? Who were key influencers that catapulted you from where you were to where you are? Sometimes, just writing down your story will help you to focus. Sometimes, charting your life's journey will bring about a revelation of your calling and your next assignment. After you have sat down to write or record your journey, answer the questions below and honestly assess where you are as it relates to your call. Nothing else in this book will be of significant value to you if this critical work isn't done. Before we can give instruction, we must give time for introspection. Before we can teach, we must give time to learn. Before we accept the new, we must be willing to process the old. This is your time to focus. This is your time to align yourself. This is your time to move toward clarity. If you don't do it for yourself, nobody else will do it for you. Take some time, and explore your own journey.

QUESTIONS FOR INTROSPECTION/
SMALL GROUP DISCUSSION

❶Although we might agree that there should be a vast difference between having a job versus fulfilling a ministry assignment, there are professional expectations attached to our weekly performance of ministry. Indeed, many of us earn our living by leading worship ministries. In view of this, how do you balance the professional and spiritual aspects of your calling to achieve optimum outcomes?

❷The four values of *Clarity, Movement, Alignment, and Focus* play a significant role in one's success. Carefully craft and define each value with your overall purpose and mission. Be sure to give and gain support from an accountability partner.

❸Do you fully recognize the difference between doing ministry and having a job? How important is making an "impact" in ministry to you? Are you doing what you are doing for purpose, or are you doing what you are doing for a paycheck? Why is "impact" a factor that distinguishes between the two?

❹It was not until I began to document my personal journey that I discovered I was destined for this career path. Take the time to outline, discuss, and document your journey. What are the interesting outcomes or threads that have aided in your current success?

❺What have you overlooked in your journey that needs to be looked at carefully (bad, indifferent, or positive) that will give you the momentum to carry out your assignment?

CHAPTER 4
Who's Really In Charge?
On pastor and musician relationships

In the last two chapters, we examined the call and the journey. In this chapter, I want to place a magnifying glass over the last 26 years of my tenure as Worship Pastor for the Mississippi Boulevard Christian Church, and focus on leadership development. As I reflect on my personal and professional development, I have seen my leadership style shift over time throughout many stages. Some of those shifts, especially in ministry, were a direct result of the relationship I had as Music Director with the Senior Pastor of said church. These stages coincide with the model Bruce Tuckman developed. He asserts, and I agree, "there are four phases in development. Each one (forming, storming, norming, performing) is necessary and inevitable in order for the team to grow, to face challenges, to tackle problems, to find solutions, to plan work, and to deliver results." As you read my stages below, think about your life, your call, and your development. Where were you formed? When did you encounter storms? When did you norm and perform? Did any of these stages repeat themselves in your life? If so, why?

FORMING (1989-1994)

When you are going through the forming stage, you develop a high dependence on your leader for guidance and direction. You take everything your leader says seriously because he or she is cultivating and nurturing you for development. When I transitioned to Memphis,

Tennessee in August of 1989, I had one primary goal when I arrived at the Blvd.: to "prove myself" as an established musician, and gain the approval of the leadership. I was only twenty-nine years old, so the truth is, I didn't have much experience to corroborate my competence. I was, in short, being formed. I wanted people to see me as a leader who took his job seriously. I wanted to be respected, appreciated, and validated. After all, I was following in the footsteps of one of the most revered musicians in all of Memphis—Mrs. Gale Jones-Murphy. Pianist and composer extraordinaire, Mrs. Gale Jones-Murphy was a prominent name within and beyond the entire Seventh Day Adventist denomination. No pressure, right? Wrong.

During this stage of formation, I had to learn to trust others. I had to learn to embrace the wonderful moments, and learn from my mistakes. I had staff members (when I first began) who were unproductive, and I chose not to groom them. I had a lot to learn, but God in the midst of my good and bad decisions, yet granted me favor. Paul sites: *"Not in your own strength for it is God who is all the while effectively at work in you, energizing and creating in you the power and desire), both to will and to work for His good pleasure and satisfaction and delight." Phil.2:13 (Amp)* My first assignment was to establish myself as a musician and gain the confidence of my pastoral leadership. I focused on scheduling, preparing, and executing special concerts (like the Christmas Concert) during the first four months of my tenure. Simultaneously, I worked hard to maintain the culture of excellence during the Sunday worship services. In addition, I had to earn the trust of my boss and CEO, Senior Pastor Dr. Alvin O. Jackson. By this time, the church was rapidly growing. Within three years of my tenure, we moved from our 1,200 seat sanctuary to a seating capacity of 2,800. One of the amazing attributes of Dr. Alvin

O'neal Jackson was his ability to connect with each member despite the vastness of our congregation. He was intentional about making others' needs, his needs (i.e. visiting the sick, blessing homes and children, providing food for needy families and charities). Hands down, Dr. Jackson had a heart for the people like no one else I had ever met. This time of forming allowed me to develop relationships, staff, musical growth, and face my deep-rooted self-esteem issues and fears.

STORMING 1995-2005

The "storming" stage came sooner than I expected. With the sudden church growth and the move to a larger facility, we did not have the chance to establish a team. Instead, we were overwhelmed by the consistent expectation to keep the consumer/congregation happy. Clarity about our purpose increased but there were plenty of uncertainties within our team. Our attendance numbers averaged (between two worship services) at over 4,000 (total), and our membership was close to 9,000. We were considered the largest Disciples of Christ congregation in the denomination and sited as one of the fastest growing churches in the mid-south. But in the midst of such a monumental growth spurt, Dr. Jackson was summoned by God's leading to take a new Senior Pastor position at the National City Christian Church in Washington, D.C. (the Mother church). *The storm had begun!!!* What would lie ahead for our congregation? What would this mean for our future leadership? There were so many questions and concerns; so much fear and distress. But, God kept us in the midst of it all.

WHAT WOULD THIS MEAN FOR OUR FUTURE LEADERSHIP? THERE WERE SO MANY QUESTIONS AND CONCERNS; SO MUCH FEAR AND DISTRESS. BUT, GOD KEPT US IN THE MIDST OF IT ALL

In the midst of this herculean loss, our music ministry emerged as a beacon of hope, courage, and unity. We would sing with confidence, "God will never leave us nor forsake us." It was God's faithfulness that kept us through the storm, and it was God's faithfulness that brought us into the next phase of the journey through the leadership of a new Senior Pastor, Dr. Frank Anthony Thomas. We repositioned ourselves, watched the storm subside, and before we knew it, we were on our way back to the top.

During this time, I also embraced a new relationship that would eventually catapult me as a musician. I was invited to become a member of the Moses Hogan Singers, a professional African American choral ensemble. Singers were selected from a small pool of talented professionals. They hailed from all around the country—primarily, New Orleans—and a large constituency sang in the Morgan State University Chorus. This opportunity inspired me as a musician and then, seemingly out of nowhere, our founder and director passed away in February of 2003. Another storm! That same year, a disgruntled group within the congregation filed a lawsuit. Needless to say, we were going through a heart wrenching and a soul-searching time for our congregation. But, our music ministry rose to the occasion once again, and summoned the church to unity and love. Essentially, the music ministry demonstrated harmony in the midst of dis-harmony. In the middle of a lawsuit, we were able to maintain a standard of grace within the church. We even completed our first recording, "LIVE @ THE BLVD" in the midst of the storm. But one of the drawbacks was that I did not learn how to take care of myself through this process. I was spiritually and physically depleted. I could feel the weight of the church being carried on the shoulders of the music ministry.

NORMING/ PERFORMING (2006-2010)

Norming: agreement and consensus largely formed among the team, who respond well to facilitation by leader. Roles and responsibilities are clear and accepted.

Performing: the team is more strategically aware: the team knows clearly why it is doing what it is doing. High degree of autonomy.

Establishing, obtaining and achieving goals are essential in this stage. In order to norm and perform well, you must obtain clarity about the vision, clarity about the mission and clarity about your church's music philosophy. How do we move towards excellence? Successful planning, communication, and a spiritual commitment to God and your pastoral team are a must! Dr. Thomas was not only a brilliant scholar. He was also intentional about restoring momentum in our congregation.

The church began to grow slowly. By this point, I had completed the Doctor of Musical Arts degree, and we had established two premiere productions 1. Christmas Concert 2. Umoja Celebration, which became regionally and nationally known events. The worship ministry began to move in tandem with the leadership and we began to gain momentum in our department. But the lawsuit ended in 2005, and the church took another hit for many reasons. Attendance and membership began to dwindle significantly, and despite our greatest efforts to revive the masses, we never really regained our footing. Pastor Thomas successfully retired in December of 2012 after 13 years of service.

RE-FORMING (2011-2014)

New leadership was assumed on Easter Sunday, 2013. Rev. J. Lawrence Turner, a young, vibrant, and stunning preacher took the helm of this historic congregation. The first year had been exciting. At the same time, it was quite interesting to see the congregational changes and the management of staff. I couldn't imagine what was happening to me: I had to begin the stages of development all over again! I couldn't imagine that I would still need to be creative after learning to work with five different pastoral leads since 1989. But I had to do it! I mastered the art of focus. I retooled extremely well, and I made things palatable for my team at the Blvd. I think this kind of flexibility is extremely important for worship directors anywhere and everywhere. After establishing your career, building relationships, and mastering the essential ingredient (of hearing from God and his people), prepare yourself to be challenged again. Never leave the posture of a student. Always be willing to learn something new. Be open to change. Give grace to new leaders the same way you would want grace to be given to you. When you do that, God will always bless you, and you will always be a blessing to others.

> ALWAYS BE WILLING TO LEARN SOMETHING NEW. BE OPEN TO CHANGE. GIVE GRACE TO NEW LEADERS THE SAME WAY YOU WOULD WANT GRACE TO BE GIVEN TO YOU.

A MORE EXCELLENT WAY

The relationship between pastoral leader and worship leader/music director can be overwhelming at first glance, but when you see this relationship through the eyes of the spirit, it will make perfect sense. This kind of spirit-led perspective is what I call *a more excellent way.* The first thing you must realize, in order to do ministry excellently, is that somebody will have to die to their agenda in order for God to be exalted with His agenda. After all of the gold microphones are handed out, and after the congregation is told to stand up honorably at the entrance of a person or personality, God wants to get glory in His house. After the arguments ensue because one singer feels like the pastor cut his song out of the service intentionally, and the pastor feels like one singer over-sang a song that should've been shorter than what they deemed the spirit wanted, remember: God wants to get glory in His house. In order to be effective, we must learn to do ministry in a more excellent way.

Over time I've had to learn the importance of forging a God-pleasing relationship with the visionary leader of the church. In order for optimal results, not only in worship but also in terms of the overall wholeness of the church, the leaders must be unified. Of course, because we are in a fallen world, and our human experience lends itself to differences of opinions, we must actualize our Christ-like walk in the midst of our differences. *This is the excellent way:* knowing when to step forward and lead, and knowing when to step backward and follow. *This is the excellent way*: having the humility to stay in your lane even though you know you can do it better. But also having the boldness to lovingly confront someone who is standing in the need of correction. *This is the excellent way:* being willing to lay our egos down at the altar, and being able to trust that God will fight for us even when we want to fight for ourselves.

Let's be honest. Egos are a major contributing factor when we consider why pastors and musicians struggle with working together. One of the ways egos can be tempered and trust can be established is by having clear roles and boundaries. This is where the rubber will meet the road. Clarity must be ascertained and communicated on every level of the leadership ladder. Frustration, mistrust, and bitterness show up when roles and boundaries are not clearly defined. I have had to learn to carefully discern, dissect, and balance different leaders based on the different boundaries they set. The music ministry must communicate for clarity, and the Senior Pastor must communicate their limitations. No one can do everything. If you micro-manage, that is a consequence of mis-trust, and if you give instructions without follow-through, that is a consequence of apathy. Both must be rectified in order for the church to embrace a more excellent way.

CONFIDENTIALITY IN LEADERSHIP

Lee Orr wrote so eloquently in his publication, T*he Church Music Handbook:* "Pastor and musician must abdicate their thrones, open themselves up to dialogue, and move from pride to partnership. Only in this way will worship regain its spiritual vigor, the congregation become empowered, and the church rise anew to face its challenge. If these two key leaders within the ministry cannot work in unity, how will they be able to lead others?"

There are three primary factors to consider when examining the relationship between music minister and pastor: *development, support and affirmation.* Successful partnerships are fully developed by clarity and honesty. Successful partnerships also exist to support one another, not compete with each other. Successful partnerships must confirm that development and support through consistent affirmation. We are a team. This is why we exist. When we cease to be a team, we create di-vision in God's house.

IF YOU TRUST ME, THEN YOU KNOW I WON'T STEP OUTSIDE OF YOUR VISION. AND IF I TRUST YOU, THEN I WILL BRING SUGGESTIONS TO THE TABLE THAT ENLIVEN YOUR VISION.

Another essential ingredient is the "rule of confidentiality." Can the music director be trusted and can the Senior Pastor be trusted? Over time, the truth of one's character will be revealed. Hopefully, truth and honesty will always win. But trust is major. If you trust me, then you know I won't step outside of your vision. And If I trust you, then I will bring suggestions to the table that enliven your vision.

COMMENTS FROM SENIOR AND WORSHIP PASTORS

During my preparation for this particular chapter, I decided to ask several pastors and musicians to share their heartfelt views on worship, relationship, and communication. Let's explore their comments:

Dr. Gina M. Stewart: Senior Pastor-Christ MB Church-Memphis, TN

"The Message and music are the "Siamese Twins" in a worship experience. Harmonious relationships between the Senior Pastor and the Minister of Music/Worship Pastor and the Music Ministry can help to facilitate the release of God's presence and lead worshippers to experience fresh encounters in the presence of the Lord."

Anonymous Musician: Dallas, Texas

"Trust your professional musician and his/her musical knowledge, taste, and wisdom. Do not micromanage him/her. That is the person to whom you must turn for making informed decisions about what music is appropriate for your congregation. Perhaps your colleague at a neighboring church has a larger membership than you do, so naturally you want to do whatever it takes to get a larger membership yourself. But do not assume that abandoning your music program and trying to emulate them is the answer.

Dr. Stacy Spencer- Senior Pastor, New Direction Christian Church. Memphis, TN.

"Be disciplined, come in early, plan out your day, and keep your Senior Pastor informed of your plans for the year. Communicate! Communicate! Communicate! Make sure the rotation of music stays fresh and balanced. The music should pave the way for the sermonic moment, not compete with it or diminish it."

Anonymous Musician: Chicago, Illinois

"Please plan ahead and get me the service information in advance. I know things will change from time to time. However, don't excuse a lack of planning as the Holy Spirit's leading. I had a pastor who would change things on me the spur of the moment, because he believed the Holy Spirit told him to make the change that morning. I believe my God is a god of organization and order. Do things happen at the last minute from time to time? Yes. However, it should not be a weekly occurrence."

Bishop T. Garrott Benjamin. Senior Pastor. Light of the World Christian Church. Indianapolis, Indiana.

"If I had one piece of advice for the musician who sincerely wants to be successful it would be this: Love your pastor because love is the foundation of trust. Once you trust, you can let go of ego and submit. This partnership, like marriage, calls for mutual submission. This will lead to both understanding and respect of each other's discipline.

Kristin Lensch Organist-Choirmaster Calvary Episcopal Church, Memphis, Tennessee

The inner sanctuary of the working relationship between clergy and musicians is found in the weekly worship planning meeting. Working together as partners in Christ, to craft meaningful worship for parishioners is an exercise in mutual respect, honesty, compromise, trust, grace, and vulnerability. Meeting weekly fosters communication and intentional care for the most important shared task – leading worship.

Anonymous Pastor: Peoria, Illinois.

"I think (church musicians) should be able to think theologically, but I also think they should think pastorally (by which I mean).... knowing what the pastoral moment is in history and in the life of a particular congregation. I think they need to have the whole picture of the service in mind. These qualities they share with the clergy. I think the things the musician brings are: the language of music, which is different from the language of the rest of the liturgy, and attention to quality "performance." A service ought to be like a symphony with themes and movements."

Rabbi Micah D. Greenstein - Senior Rabbi, Temple Israel - Memphis, Tennessee

"Music is the language of prayer. It is the bridge between and within every section of the worship service. As Senior Rabbi, I meet with my worship team the preceding Wednesday before every weekend Sabbath service. I let the cantorial soloist know the theme of my sermon so that the anthem or hymn prior to the homily compliments and magnifies the message. A trusting and empowering relationship between the pastor and musician, in my view, is the most critical element in creating a rich worship experience for the congregation. When that relationship is seamless and stress-free, the service sings on its own and the Oneness of God is modeled by the oneness of pastor and musician."

Anonymous Pastor:

"I want the musicians to know how challenging it is to write a sermon. Please, please, please tell church musicians that preachers do not appreciate it when the musician leaves during the sermon."

Clark W. Joseph. Minister of Worship & Creative Arts, St. John Church. Grand Prairie, TX.

Worship - *a lifestyle of worship is required to lead others in worship. Prayer is essential to the success of leading others into experiencing God. Every service should have a general theme from which everything flows. Getting the Pastor's sermon text and title will help in determining the music that will be selected.*

Relationship - *The relationship between the Pastor and Musician is similar to a marriage. The two must strive to give 100% to achieve a successful union. Because no two people are perfect, each will fall short. Because of the call of God on each other's lives and loyalty, the relationship can remain healthy. The Pastor is the CEO. The Musician's job is to support the Pastor and the ministry so that he is presented in excellence at all times. Learn the Pastor's likes and dis-likes and then acquiesce accordingly. Bring creative ideas that are low cost, but have high impact. Always be willing to go above and beyond the call of duty.*

Communication - *Good communication comes from spending time with and learning the Pastor. Learn the Pastor's preferred mode of communication: email/text/phone call/face to face. Determine the best time to communicate with the Pastor. Always be brief and succinct, thereby maximizing communication time. Always be attentive to everything the*

Pastor says, as well as his thought processes. Seek to learn the Pastor's heart and respond to situations accordingly."

Rev. Eddie A. Robinson Director of Worship and Arts - Springfield Baptist Church - Conyers, GA.

"Pastor and Minister of Music must be connected together in the heart and in the ministry. Healthy dialogue is important throughout the work relationship. Great salaries, great benefits, great facilities do not take the place of a great relationship with the pastor. Pastors should minister to their staff and not just through them. You are the pastor. We work to complete your ministry and not compete with your ministry.

PASTORS SHOULD MINISTER TO THEIR STAFF AND NOT JUST THROUGH THEM.

Rev. Dr. Charles E. Goodman, Jr. :Senior Pastor/Teacher, Tabernacle Baptist Church, Augusta, GA.

"Worship is a time for the people of God to come together as one body to glorify the wonderful name of our Lord and Savior. During this special and sacred time, the pastor and the musician must communicate effectively so the Spirit of the lord can be felt and magnified through song, praise, and the message. Both the pastor and the musician must work together for the common goal of delivering the Word of God. This "sacred synergy" between pastor and musician is what invites the faithful worshipping community into the manifested presence of God."

Anonymous Musician: Seattle, Washington:

"We church musicians love serving the Lord and the church. We love serving the people of our churches. We are interested in helping support

sacred texts, and we would like clergy to give theological interpretations of Bible readings, so that we may help choose music that supports these texts. We would also like to know sermon topics in advance, and any salient points the clergy would like all who hear the readings and sermons to understand and remember. We would like a working relationship with mutual respect among the vestry (or senior management volunteers), staff, and clergy at a church.

Dr. Eugene Gibson, Senior Pastor, Olivet Baptist Church. Memphis, TN.

"There are probably no two more ego-charged and competition-driven performance assignments than the twin calls of the Senior Minister and the Head Musician. Both are the objects of the adoration and adulation of the people and both handle the "Holy." Their healthy relationship of respect and trust is key in order that their expected conflict does not upstage the intended work of god. It is a must that seminaries recognize the discipline to graduate from their institution without at least basic classes in the other discipline. This should include but not be limited to: Music Theory, Intro to Theology, Old Testament."

Dr. Gabriel C. Statom, Director of Music, Second Presbyterian Church, Memphis, TN

In my years of music ministry, I have had several different scenarios and levels of relationships to the pastor. In the seven years I have been at Second Presbyterian in Memphis, the structure for worship planning has evolved, particular in how the trust is built between pastor and musician. Currently, our senior minister plans his sermons out a year in advance and puts them in a spreadsheet with the entire year laid out, including *sermon title, scripture and with the liturgical dates. So, with this, I can plan choral music plenty far in advance. For each individual service, I work with an associate pastor who is in charge of the liturgical aspects of the service to plan about three weeks in advance of each service. The communication with the senior pastor is still very open and I have access to him whenever needed. We try to meet one on one every month or two, or as needed. Because the church staff is so large, developing relationships with the assistant pastors has also been important. The relationships vary with each, but because of the importance of music, they, especially the senior pastor, has been very intent in building a good working relationship with the music staff. I have found most importantly that the relationship building is best for developing trust.*

Paul Vasile- Free Lance and Church Music Consultant. New York, New York

"I want worship planning to be a mutually creative process, which allows us both to bring our best to God and to our congregation. I appreciate when my pastor shares the musical experiences that they have outside of worship with me (e.g. listening to live or even recorded music). They help me to understand how he/she names what is meaningful and beautiful to them. I am grateful for a pastor who has offered the freedom and encouragement to create new pieces of music for our congregation. Permission-giving has been a valuable part of our relationship."

Dr. Alvin O'neal Jackson. Senior Pastor-Park Avenue Christian Church. New York. New York.

"I want a musician who understands first and foremost that they are involved in ministry. The work is not primarily about producing a great

performance, but about leading the congregation in the worship and praise of God. I want a musician who can read, not just music, but who can read people and read the theological and musical heritage of the congregation. I want a musician who is passionate about their work and who lives, loves God, loves people, loves good preaching, loves worship, and loves me. What's love got to do with it? Everything!!"

Roberto L. Burton. Minister of Music. New Jerusalem Baptist Church. Harvest, AL. Band Director and Staff Organist at Oakwood University. Huntsville, AL.

"The relationship between the Pastor and the musician is an important relationship in the life of the church universal. No matter the denomination, the pastor and the musician, must be a cohesive bond that flows through the pew, so that the message of Jesus Christ can be proclaimed through word, and through song. Worship preparation for both the pastor and the musician is a key element. The first step is to ask God for guidance.

As a musician, no matter the instrument, the next lesson is to be on time. So many musicians miss this milestone, and then expect to be paid what they think they are worth when they have missed the most important element, timeliness. Before we touch the actual music aspect of it all, next are the little things. Patch cables, extension cords, batteries, strings, etc. The little things you need to make rehearsal and/or service pleasant without forgetting the essentials.

Lastly, learn the music. Whether its sheet music or and mp3, just learn it. If you don't have time to learn it, then create a Nashville chord chart and use that until your performance. You will have it memorized by then. In dealing with the relationship factor, before entering my current assignment at St. John AME, I read the first 15 pages of the pastor's Ph.D. dissertation online at www.academic.edu. It told me a lot about who he was as an educator. As a preacher my first sermon with Dr. Patrick Clayborn was in Birmingham, AL. After the sermon was over the congregation was still rejoicing. The platform participants were trying to move on with the rest of the service. All I remember is, seeing my pastor take off running. My hands went up in shock and then I said, "self, aren't you the one on the organ?" The rest is history. The relationship I share with my pastor is a strong one because; he shares the word of God in such a tangible way."

I pray these contributions have blessed you. I am honored to know such great minds—both musician and pastor alike—who have tirelessly dedicated hours of sacrifice to their craft. In addition to the above contributors, I have also been privileged to serve under dynamic pastors during my entire career, and for this I am grateful. It is from this pool of experience that I would like to give some final words of encouragement to both the senior pastor and music director.

> IN ORDER TO SERVE THE CHURCH TO THE BEST OF OUR ABILITY, TRUST MUST BE A NON-NEGOTIABLE.

Our relationship, as a team, is crucial to the edification of God's church. In order to serve the church to the best of our ability, trust must be a non-negotiable. The pastor must trust his key musician, and the musician (or worship director) must trust the pastor. Every church operates differently, but the roles must be respected and the expectations must be communicated.

Often, it is the lack of communication, not money or skill, that tears churches apart. The same is true with the relationship between the senior leader and the musical director. Each person must clearly identify their role, their philosophies on music, and the objective of this team. When in doubt, revisit the vision. When in doubt, ask before you assume. Behind closed doors, the pastor must trust the director of worship. Behind closed doors, the director of worship must trust the pastor. Otherwise, it will show in the public eye. People will be able to see what you don't say. People will be able to discern that you don't like your pastor (or vice versa). No matter how you craft it or try to hide it, people will see the dysfunction and call it out.

If you ever encounter a "disconnection" between senior leader and musical director—perhaps the pastor isn't cooperative, perhaps the music director is narcissistic—remember that your first call is to please God. Your first assignment is to carry out God's will for this house. When you experience or encounter friction on any level, my word of wisdom is to walk closer with God. The closer you walk with God, the more likely God will show you favor even in the midst of a difficult leadership situation.

Another word of wisdom that I will give to both pastor and musician is this: know when to step forward and lead, and know when to back up and follow. As senior pastor, there are some blindspots that you can't see, but your director of worship will see. Trust him or her to carry their weight. As director of worship, there are some things that your senior pastor can do better than you. Trust them to lead the church in the direction that God is unctioning them to go in. Sometimes, you will have to swallow your pride, and give your superior an idea in private, that he or she will take the credit for in public. Don't get upset when you don't get acknowledged. Remember that all good and perfect gifts come from above—so even the song you recommended, or the scripture you suggested, or the guest preacher you invited—those ideas stemmed from a good God who downloaded them into your spirit.

If you learn to manage the dance between leading sometimes and following at other times, then you won't major on a minor. If you learn to respect your leader and protect your leader in public, and then confront your leader in private, you will never have to worry about private matters becoming public. Remember the words written in James 1: *be quick to hear, slow to speak.* Sometimes, we talk too quickly. Sometimes, we make assumptions. That is why clarity and communication are of primary importance. If you offend your leader, apologize. If you offend your director, apologize. Never get too high and mighty that you can't say, "I'm sorry for offending you." There is a difference between saying, "If I offended you...I'm sorry," and "I'm sorry for offending you." Language is important. One takes ownership of the wrongdoing; the other implies that you are free from responsibility but you are going to say I'm sorry anyway. Mature leaders will own it. Mature leaders will take responsibility.

And while we are on the subject of owning your words, leaders... please, make sure that you are honest about what you want, and not saying things you don't mean. *Let me explain by giving a realistic example.* In my experience, I've heard many senior leaders say that they want "diverse worship" or they want "a first class music ministry." But when I introduced new styles of music to embrace a more diverse musical repertoire, they were hesitant to approve it. Many people do not realize how much work is needed to make their dream come true. Shifts take work. Shifts require consistency, methods, and support. If this is what we want, then we must be willing to do the work. Leaders, both pastors and musicians, must be honest about what they want. If a senior pastor is too egotistical or insecure to share the stage with someone who is more gifted, then they need to honestly admit that they are not ready to hire superlative musicians. Self-awareness and truth are critical to a seamless organization. Some truth may be hard to admit. Sometimes we have biases, prejudices, unmet needs, and unfinished work that God needs to do in us, but if we are going to work together with other visionary leaders, then we can't tell them to execute according to a vision for which we are not ready to embrace.

.IF A SENIOR PASTOR IS TOO EGOTISTICAL OR INSECURE TO SHARE THE STAGE WITH SOMEONE WHO IS MORE GIFTED, THEN THEY NEED TO HONESTLY ADMIT THAT THEY ARE NOT READY TO HIRE SUPERLATIVE MUSICIANS.

Be honest with yourself, be honest with your God, and be honest with each other. Before anything is done, meet. Talk. Learn to love one another outside of the tasks you do. It is very hard to work that closely with someone, week in and week out, if they are a stranger to you. Your commitment to seeing your leader as a person, and not just as a work-for-hire, is crucial. Remember: everybody wants to be useful; but nobody wants to be used. These are the nuggets of development that every worship director/music director will need to master.

This chapter title asks a crucial question: Who is in charge? Is the pastor in charge, or is the music director in charge? Is the pastor in charge of the sermon, but the music director is in charge of the song? Who is in charge? My answer would be quite simple: God. God is in charge of both. God rules his church. The pastor stewards it. God rules his sound. The music director stewards it. All of us are called to watch over God's vision until he comes back. God is the leader of His church—and it is his way, or no way at all. When we fully embrace that, we will be able to work together in harmony, peace, and joy!

QUESTIONS FOR INTROSPECTION/
SMALL GROUP DISCUSSION

❶What stage would you consider your current relationship with you and the Senior Pastor or Leadership? Is there good communication? Is it pretentious? Can you both communicate freely? When you meet with your Senior Pastor or Leadership, is there a considerable amount of prayer prior to moving on with an agenda?

❷It's important to develop a network of "godly" musical comrades to hold you accountable, especially in relationship to your Senior Pastor. Persons that will give you "sound" advice in conflict management areas in particular. Can you readily identify those persons? If so, how accountable are you to them?

❸Can you honestly say that you and your pastor coincide with the vision of the Worship and Arts? Or that you are in sync with his/her visionary leadership?

❹Most "creative types," have extremely strong personalities, especially when it comes to their personal brand, gifts, and execution. How well do you swing into the rhythm of the Senior Pastor, and allow them to lead and be the "pastor" and not cross the lines? We talk the talk but how do we walk the walk?

❺How do we really agree to disagree with the leadership, respectfully? How do we gingerly express that they might be moving in error, and not risk the loss of our job? Do we receive chastisement well? Can we as "creative types" really be "PASTORED?"

CHAPTER 5
The Demand for Excellence: No Compromise

Personal Philosophy of Music Ministry:

In an effort to model excellence in our overall worship music ministry endeavors, the leadership must fully define and give clarity to his/her personal philosophy. Our philosophy of church music is most noticeably seen in the way in which we carry out ministry in the real world, for our beliefs inform all ministry decisions. What I believe and experience about God carries out poignantly in my selection and leadership process in worship. In addition to my personal beliefs about God, what are my personal beliefs about the approach to worship ministry (i.e. structure, pursuit of excellence, strategies, and implementations, etc.)? In order to lead with clarity, precision and power, you must develop a philosophy that includes knowledge of your church's music history.

Stories told by musicians for centuries about the beauty and power of music have been validated in our time by the behavior of people so deeply affected by that beauty and power that they have been known to walk unaware into the path of a moving vehicle. Only tiny wires hanging silently from their ears, and eyes apparently insensitive to their physical surroundings reveal the human being's state of enchantment of invisible vibratory patterns of sounds. But electronics will never give them the thrill of singing music themselves, when sound vibrates throughout their entire bodies. Fortunately, singing is an experience that churches have nourished and passed on for centuries, even multiplying it to include the joy of music-making with others, especially in the singing of congregational singing. **(Dr. Carol Doran "Teaching Your Congregation About the Church's Music" - Paper)**

Throughout the history of the African American church, music has been of vital importance not only to the liturgy but to the very existence of our worship experience. The historical premise of the "secret" meeting worship houses for slaves indicated the importance of identifying our own personal worship culture in an effort to maintain a sense of stability. Deprivation of our human rights prompted us to be ingenious in our planning in the following: 1. Worshipful location 2. Worship style 3. Sanctity of beliefs.

Worshipful Location: According to Miles Fisher, "Slaves needed the comfort of group fellowship in order to condition themselves to slave situations. The African cult had trained Negroes to dress their finest for worship. In Africa, they wore cotton, silk, and velvet beautifully ornamented with embroidery and jewelry of gold and silver" *(Negro Slave Songs in the United States).* Henceforth, we have cultivated many of the principles passed down from our forefathers (i.e. dress, celebratory worship styles in music and preaching, etc.), to convey our appreciation of deliverance to hope and freedom. The sacredness of our established places of worship has waned over the years in an effort to galvanize more of the European style based "unchurched" approach. Seemingly the "unchurched" in addition to "millenials," are in search for the "truth," about who God is. They're not for the most part, concerned or looking for familiarity. The real quest is for integrity and truth. What is the truth about God? I believe that the sacredness of our spaces of worship, without any of the prescribed "gimmicks,", but not necessarily essentials for a valued worship space—must be restored. I believe that the African American worship culture does not have to necessarily "dumb-down" or emulate the European trends to become relevant. Of course, I'm not biased. I love all varied styles of worship, but my deepest appreciation and cultivation has been instilled within the African American tradition, and I endeavor to be the best at its delivery. That is why the church is in need of Levites who have a passion for the delivery and power of excellence in worship ministry.

Worship Style: As it pertains to the origination of worship within the Black Church, it is imperative that we carefully delineate the how and the why of the African American experience. In the 18th and 19th century, missionaries sought to proselytize the slaves. As slaves converted to Christianity, some chose to worship in a manner that reflected the practices of their European counterparts; while others chose to worship in a manner that coincided with their African heritage. As a result of the demonstrative behavior that characterized this new form of worship, style, and song, whites and some blacks were adamantly opposed to this form of worship. For instance, a white Methodist minister, John F. Watson in 1819, published a book titled *Methodist Error or Friendly Christian Advice to Those Methodists Who Indulge in Extravagant Religious Emotions and Bodily Exercises.* In it, he states the following: "We have too, a growing evil, in the practice of singing in our places of public and society worship, merry airs, adapted from old songs, to hymns of our composing often miserable as poetry, and senseless as matter." There are far too many historical attachments that not only support our tie to the worship style of our forefathers, but continue to show how we have combined both African and European trend styles to make a cohesive and unique expression.

I propose that African-American worship styles must lend themselves to a diversity of preferences, ranging from blended, traditional, and contemporary styles. As an extension of the baby boomer era (which lends itself to a more traditional style base) I love what I grew up listening to. But at the same time, I remain obstinate about my conviction as it relates to the importance of blended worship. I am not opposed to either style, however, my passion and forte exist within the context of musical diversity. The scripture states emphatically, "They that worship Him, must worship Him in spirit and in truth" (John 4:24). I'm not saying that we should formulate our opinions and methods to the absence of the presence of God. But I am saying that one's gifts, passions, values and methods of successful execution (from the academy, exposure, and generational depth) must be taken into account. As a result, one's worship tradition, space, and style will remain insignificant if, at the end of the worship event, transformation does not happen.

Sanctity of Beliefs: The importance and value of one's philosophy and beliefs about God will permeate every experience. The black worship experience "is connected with black life, and characterized by a religious sense inseparable from the suffering that determined it." The beliefs of black worship originated and "cannot be separated from our African heritage on the one hand and American slavery and Christianity on the other. Black worship was created and formed in the context of American slavery as African slaves sought to create meaning in a completely alien and oppressive environment. In order to keep a measure of sanity in a completely alien and oppressive environment, slaves had to fashion a theological system of beliefs and create a worship style that did not destroy them physically and mentally." *(From: Readings in African American Church Music and Worship. Volume 2) "Black Worship: A Historical Theological Interpretation" by James H.Cone).*

As a worship pastor, my beliefs help create and establish the culture of worship for the congregation I am called to lead. Those beliefs and philosophies are shaped out of the relational and personal experiences of who God is. Do we view God as a taskmaster, or as a loving father full of grace? Do we view him as a narcissist or a just judge? Are His attributes being experienced in the lives of those that lead and teach us? If not, the void will be unavoidable in our planning, teaching and execution. The old adage remains true: "You can't go where you've never been. You can't teach what you've never experienced." If I've never mourned, then I would never know how to experience God as a comforter." Etc. Once those beliefs have been consistent, shaped, and honed,

> "YOU CAN'T GO WHERE YOU'VE NEVER BEEN. YOU CAN'T TEACH WHAT YOU'VE NEVER EXPERIENCED."

then our communication will be very clear and not waver. With that in mind, have a working knowledge of one's worship tradition, and one's own individual skillset (i.e. what one believes about church music) is of prime importance. In order to do this with an effective rubric in mind, the following questions should be considered: how do you express your own unique place in church music? What is your calling? How do you deal with change? What are your non-negotiables? For every worship director who is developing a philosophy for their department or ministry, non-negotiables must be carefully defined. This will become your rubric for truth.

MY NON-NEGOTIABLES

Of the many non-negotiables that I have as it pertains to music ministry, here are three that are unanimous and ubiquitous, not matter the place I am called to serve.

1) Believe in the transforming power of the word of God.

2) Believe in music as the tool that must be consistently

communicated with clarity, vibrancy, excellence, and power.

3) Reject sub-standard functionality and expression in church worship music.

My non-negotiables are not just my personal philosophy, it is also the rubric I use to determine who will collaborate with and work with me. Once I became clear about my own non-negotiables, then I began to move with clarity, passion and empowerment. In the same way, as you begin to grow, develop, and deepen your well of knowledge, your philosophy and passion will change as seasons change. However, the clarity of the call and the initial foundational premise should always remain the same...EXCELLENCE UNTO THE LORD... SOLI DEO GLORIA.

HIRING COMPETENT STAFF:

This is a very delicate topic—this issue of hiring competent staff—members; and I must be completely honest with you, I must admit: I have not mastered this area yet. However, there has been significant growth in terms of my clarity in the following areas:

1. Prayerful consideration of the desired position and candidate:

2. Skillset of applicant

3. Functionality, chemistry and DNA of applicant with team, participants, and church.

4. Clarity of Job Description.

I strongly believe that the aforementioned areas have aided in my success and growth as a music director. I recall a conversation with one of the team members on our Human Resources Committee. She shared with me this nugget of wisdom: "a fast hire can be the worst hire." Of course there are several variables that come into play with hiring staff, and the amount of time to segue between roles is almost always inconvenient and inopportune. Nevertheless, you must do your homework and resist the temptation to hire in order to meet a need. Hire to fulfill purpose. Pay attention and ask the right questions, because most often, the real individual will not materialize at the interview; the real individual will show up after their actual performance and personality is challenged and examined over time. For me, hiring competent staff is a non-negotiable. For you, it may be necessary to investigate what you mean by competent. Does that mean they are musically trained from a professional institution of higher learning? Does that mean they are gifted with instruments, and effective communicators with people? Are they conceited or humble? Do they know the Lord, or do they just know how to play? Do they just want this job for the salary, or do they want to do ministry? Your non-negotiables are extremely important if you're going to do leadership well.

THE GRINDHOUSE

The "Grit and Grind' slogan was created by Tony Allen. It used to be a bit of a joke, but now it's a style of play that defines the Memphis Grizzlies and has led to their home arena affectionately being called, "THE GRINDHOUSE." I would like to utilize this same slogan as a metaphor for the climate I try to maintain for my rehearsals, be it personal, church, workshop, or special events. In my opinion, everybody is here to participate. This is a grindhouse. That means, each chorus member should leave the rehearsal setting: *1. EDIFIED 2. EDUCATED and 3.*

EXHAUSTED. Let me explain what I mean by each word briefly.

Edified:

As leaders, we must prepare ourselves emotionally, physically, mentally, and most importantly, spiritually, prior to joining dedicated lay members. As Pastor Claudette Copeland shared with me many years ago, "Leo, always work from the overflow." I have learned that working from the "overflow" comes as a result of my continuous and daily relationship with Jesus Christ. It may sound redundant, but the more spiritually fueled I am, the better chorus members can receive instruction. Even learning the most difficult passages of a wide variety of music, I've seen how my decision to surrender to Him, will help me to work with them even better.

Edification, therefore, is an individual experience. It requires "intellectual, moral, and spiritual improvement: enlightenment." In essence, edification is designed to help you. That has been a goal of mine for more than 20 years. I want to see individuals empowered by the presence of the Lord when they fully engage with the *why; why is it important to sing with a different timbre and tone when singing Handel's, "Coronation Anthem?" Why is it important to articulate with a certain dialect for a Negro Spiritual, or to give a gusty, robust and soulful sound when rendering a Smallwood gospel rendition?* Not only is the interpretation of the music significant, but participants must also be fully engaged in and keenly aware of the spiritual implications of that particular piece. We must render music out of our experience and relationship with God, and that can't happen without self-edification.

Education:

Not only is the rehearsal setting a place of connectivity, edification, and empowerment, it should also be a place of enlightenment and education. From congregational hymns to praise and worship selections; from Anthems and/or Spirituals to the highly spirited, or gospel ballads rendered, there should be some brief dialogue about the composer, arranger, style, etc. This gives the chorus participant and musicians more clarity and insight as it relates to the lyrics. The why, how, and when, are essentials for a key performance. Just recently, as our chorus was learning the wonderfully arranged NETTLETON- TUNE, "Come Thou Fount" arranged by Mack Wilberg, something interesting happened. At the onset, I assigned one of the altos to gather information on the hymn-tune and this particular hymn setting. By assigning a chorus member, I accomplished two things:

1. A fresh voice that chorus members readily received. Not hearing the conductor with all of the information helped the chorus members to, one day, envision themselves as participants and not just recipients.

2. Empower a committed member of the chorus. He or she must be able to follow through on assignments, and gain full buy-in from their colleagues and peers. Never underestimate your chorus. People enjoy and want to be a part of something that is structured, organized, informative, and has momentum.

Exhausted:
Being "exhausted" has nothing to do with the time parameters of the rehearsal setting. It has more to do with the amount of energy put into the rehearsal setting. Later, I will disclose how I structure rehearsals and how I strategically plan and accomplish goals. However, it is important to first

realize that 75 to 80% of our chorus members are coming to rehearsal from jobs, where they have already given the best part of their day. They already come exhausted. It really takes clever leadership to engage the chorus into learning new anthems, Spirituals, or any piece of music repertoire after working a full day at their job site. However, the chorus conductor/ lead must think cleverly about how to get things done without wasting time. If you want to turn a volunteer off immediately, come into the rehearsal unprepared. Stumble over notes and give incorrect voice parts. If you do that, I guarantee you: your rehearsal will turn in to slow-agonizing death. If the Conductor does not have the acuity necessary to prepare before rehearsal, then do not take up the choruses time learning the repertoire while standing in front of the chorus.

> IF YOU WANT TO TURN A VOLUNTEER OFF IMMEDIATELY, COME INTO THE REHEARSAL UNPREPARED. STUMBLE OVER NOTES AND GIVE INCORRECT VOICE PARTS. IF YOU DO THAT, I GUARANTEE YOU: YOUR REHEARSAL WILL TURN IN TO SLOW-

Having discussed the essentials of edification, education and exhaustion, let's think through some of the most important questions that I believe every director will need to consider:

I. How do you begin your rehearsals?

The tone of your rehearsal must be clearly set prior to their entrance into the rehearsal room. Dr. Judy Bowers, during a workshop at St. Olaf's College, shared "chorus members should feel good about the music they are learning and their execution of that music." That means all music scores, lyrics, sharpened no. 2 pencils, communication and sign-in sheets should be strategically laid out on the prep table in the hall area outside of the actual rehearsal room.

Chorus members are reminded through prior email communication of the importance of stopping by that table and making sure they are fully equipped with the materials needed for the rehearsal.

In an effort to achieve optimal results from rehearsals, it is of utmost importance that I spend time carefully planning each "movement" of the rehearsal. I take the time to draft/calculate a "rehearsal cover" sheet form. Within this form I will craft my rehearsal goals for the particular rehearsal within the allotted time frame of 2 hours. Speaking of which, it is imperative that rehearsals start and end on time as expected by those that are in attendance. If I need extra time, I will make sure that I grant chorus members a minimum of one week's notice. If I honor their time, they will honor mine. Below I will calculate a rehearsal agenda/format:

Prayer/Scripture Study:
Normally, I may start the prayer and study portion five minutes earlier than the actual start time of the rehearsal. The majority of chorus members are usually in place, and this gives the opportunity to really set the tone of the rehearsal. It is essential, especially when involved in the work of the church, that our rehearsals be carefully and intentionally centered around prayer and the study of scripture. I believe that starting the rehearsal with prayer concerns, scripture reading, and singing, assists the chorus participant and the leader to bring all thoughts in, and with intentionality, articulate with full awareness the purpose for which we have gathered. I carefully craft the opening prayers, scriptures, etc. as a time to give God praise for another opportunity to worship, learn, and gather. This is not the time for sharing bereavements, acknowledgements of persons suffering with a variety of maladies, etc. The final prayer will address all

of these concerns. As I have learned the importance of being in sync with the movement of the Holy Spirit, I make room for the promptings of the Holy Spirit. If prayer is needed in the middle of the rehearsal, we make room and move accordingly. The more sensitive I am to the needs of the people I serve, the more pliable they become to my requests. In addition, I don't usually utilize the same individuals to lead and close in prayer. The rehearsal setting must be designed as a "safe" place for persons to feel comfortable in praying, sharing, and often times sharing with their comrades in the kingdom. Our participants want to be heard and cared for just like any other person in the congregation.

Greeting:
Most rehearsals will begin and/or end with some type of "greeting" or "blessing" the persons whom you minister/sing with on a weekly basis. This gives regular attendees as well a newcomers an opportunity to become more acquainted, and also, to experience the power of the "touch." I deem it necessary that we carefully embrace, or touch the shoulder of our neighbor, in a wholesome way and environment.
When we genuinely express how grateful we are to share in this wonderful opportunity again, to sing praises to God, it is a powerful tool to embrace.

Warm-up:
I believe that most choirs, via professional, church, school, community, etc. need to take time to warm up. I tend to believe as most conductors, that the vocal warm-up should take place early on before you are in the throes of the rehearsal repertoire. There are many approaches. My approach is to cover three main vocal areas, and add other essentials as needed depending on the repertoire covered:

Range:
The majority of my chorus members are 40+, with a drastic jump to several who are in their mid-twenties. So it calls for intentionality in planning vocally for the rehearsal. It is important to calculate warm-ups that are vocally safe, and will carefully stretch the range of the voice. I make sure that voices are not pushed beyond their capacity, but are carefully and methodically challenged to stretch. I keep in mind that most chorus participants, are coming from an exhaustive day at work, where they have utilized their voices most-times quite harshly. Therefore, a few exercises that move us into broadening ranges would be essential first, such as humming:

Ex.
5 4 3   2 1 (quarter notes) modulate half steps starting on D Major ascending up to Db
Major (4/4 tempi)

1 3 5 3 1 (6/8) quarter note, eighth, quarter, eighth, quarter (modulate half-steps,
descending).

I tell chorus members to pretend that an egg is inside of the mouth, and the lips are touching, which should produce a buzzing sensation and open up the vocal folds.

I highly recommend Kenneth Jennings, *Sing Legato: a Collection of Original Studies in Vocal Production and Musicianship*. It is a comprehensive vocal resource "that provides for the director and choral participant some vocal materials that are adaptable to various levels of vocal development." As a part of my weekly quest of "educating" our chorus, I am intentional about covering sight-reading regularly. *I strongly suggest, Successful Sight-Singing, Book 1 and 2.* It is a comprehensive and creative step-by-step approach to sight singing, and it is yet challenging and fun all at the same time.. Your chorus will love it!

Sectionals:

I get quite a bit accomplished with sectional rehearsals. When working on a particular musical piece, it allows me to carefully craft the goal. I utilize sectionals only as needed for particular pieces, and utilize only qualitative leaders to cover. Person's leading sectionals are clear as to markings (i.e. dynamics, phrasing, articulations, etc.) and the expectation.

II. How do you end your rehearsals?

As much as possible, rehearsals should end on a "high point." Meaning, you should end on something that is familiar, or liked by the chorus; something they sing with passion. I deem this as necessary in particular when the majority of the rehearsal has been dedicated towards new music, and a variety of several challenging pieces. How the rehearsal ends is as significant, if not more, than the beginning. Most times for the lay-person participating, the ending is what will be held close to their memory. Announcements are usually placed in the middle of the rehearsal, but not in great length.. The Communication guide should contain all information and updates. It should not be repeated verbatim. The finale of the rehearsal always ends with chorus members sharing particular prayer requests and other needed reports of victory that need to be shared for the encouragement of the body as a whole. After the closing prayer, I intentionally encourage members to embrace two or three individuals, and thank their seated partner for sharing in the rehearsal.

III. How do you plan for rehearsals?

Planning for rehearsals takes on a life of its own. Usually, the day of the rehearsal, I try not to involve myself as much as possible with meetings, etc. I need to pour all of my energy into ensuring that I am clear and prepared for a thorough rehearsal. I am a proponent of wise, thoughtful and detailed preparation. I carefully follow a detailed form as such (Below is a rough outline. When sectionals are not needed, we forge ahead with an alternative plan).

6:55p.m. Scripture/Prayer (Nedra Anderson, facilitator)
*I may suggest scripture texts, to be in sync with the upcoming sermon or sermon series. Prayer will also be constructed around the theme as necessary.

7:00p.m. – 7:10p.m. Warm-up (Leo Davis, facilitator)
*Warm-ups depend upon the particular repertoire to be dealt with. However, I always include work on three areas: 1. Vocal Development 2. Tone 3. Range

7:10p.m. – 7:55p.m. Sectionals (Sop and Alto- Claudette Lehew, Tenors and Bass- Leo Davis)
** Facilitators are made fully aware of repertoire coverage and expectations. It is imperative that facilitators of sectionals are clear to reinforce all phrasing, articulation, dynamic markings , etc.

7:56p.m. – 8:55p.m. Combined (Leo Davis, facilitator)

Usually as chorus members "rejoin" together (SATB), brief announcements will occur for about three (3) minutes and we will then move into the rehearsal. Again, the majority of needed information (i.e. choral unit quarterly schedule, uniforms, and other significant details, inclusive of celebrations are inserted in the guide.)

Planning for the rehearsal in as much detail as possible is essential to avoid any unnecessary snafu's. There are occasions where things don't go as planned, or there will be a wonderful visitation from the "Holy Spirit," Himself. That may come at any moment of the rehearsal. However, it is most essential that the "execution" of the rehearsal be carried forth. It takes clarity of the call from God, and a personality that can engage and invite lay-persons and professional musicians alike to be trained and shifted to new levels of expectation, in order to succeed. Thirdly, a well-rounded background and experience are needed in order for participants to have the respect and trust in the leadership to get the job done.

In my execution of the rehearsal planning, I am a stickler for persons arriving after we have begun the rehearsal. Once rehearsals convene, latecomers are to always wait at the door entryway until acknowledged to enter. It lessens the need for distractions in the rehearsal setting. Allowing latecomers or individuals who randomly decide to get up and get water or bathroom breaks to return at-will, can break concentration. "Acknowledged entries" are always less distracting and disruptive, and it tends to encourage persons to be on time.

IV. How much is reasonable to expect to accomplish in a rehearsal?
Due to the fact that I carefully plan out with much detail each rehearsal,
I would have to say that 85% of the time, the goals are met. Allow me
to refer back to the sectionals and learning new repertoire. While most of
our "volunteer" church choir members are not advanced sight-readers,
or let alone, basic sight readers, that should not be justification for not
learning repertoire. As I stated earlier, I strongly suggest utilization of
the Successful Sight-Singing, Books 1 and 2 (A Creative, Step by Step
Approach) by Nancy Telfer. We cover three or four lessons a week, and
it is quite engaging for all. However, I think it is also necessary to invest
into purchasing/creating mp3 files, or tapes with parts, that are musically
accurate. I personally don't have the time, energy, or focus, to labor with
rehearsal/practice recordings any more. There are several wonderful
options that are not too expensive, but certainly worth the investment.
For example, I am avid supporter of "Choral Tracks" (info@choraltracks.
com). Mr. Matthew Curtis does remarkable work and is faithful to the
particular genre and style, precise rhythms, accompaniment provided,
and stellar vocal parts by Mr. Curtis, himself. I said that to emphasize
that I can now hold each individual chorus participant liable for taking
responsibility of the designated music. Weekly expectations are on the
communication guides, and they are forewarned of "quartet singing,"
as a follow-up. Now, I know that some might say, "Well, this is not a
professional chorus, and we certainly aren't paid, so you cannot hold lay-
persons at such a high standard." It's interesting when I get those kinds
of responses, yet those same individuals will go to an 8 hour job and
give their absolute best to a secular career, and not deem their identified
call to kingdom building worth the same fervor, tenacity and dedication.
We probably would not have as much mediocre music in our churches,

if we weren't so complacent about our approach. I'm not saying that all churches should function at the same level, however I believe that whatever genre is presented, it should be with a sense of pride and caliber. If we glorify God with our best, then His people will be edified.

V. Within a rehearsal, how much time do you spend on any given song? How much is too much/too little?

The length of time spent per selection depends on a number of factors:
- the skill level of your chorus
- Identifying the weak sections
- the level of difficulty of a particular piece
- the number of pieces allotted for the rehearsal
- the energy level of the chorus

The Skill Level of Your Chorus:
If you have an aging chorus (as most churches do), or a chorus that does not retain parts, I tend to work in smaller sections, and push them to record their rehearsals via smart devices, along with mp3 files (if knowledgeable). There is absolutely nothing wrong with referring to a "good" performance of a particular piece. It's important that the chorus is assessed quickly: 1. Balance of each section, in particular the number of male voices. 2. Range classification over all choruses.

Identification of Weak Sections:
This year, I intentionally made it mandatory for all participants in the chorus to have a private "hearing" with me personally. I took chorus members through a level of vocal warm-up exercises, tested each

individuals level of hearing recall and pitch identification, followed by sight reading levels. I never worry about making the standard too high because whether we realize it or not, chorus members at our church want to be challenged.

Level of Difficulty:
I have sometimes chosen repertoire that would be ideal for a Christmas Concert in July, because of the balance of men I presume will participate; only to find out in mid-October, that 3 of my prize baritones will have surgery, job shift changes to nights, and other personal problems. Let me offer some advice—ALWAYS KEEP A SPARE IN YOUR BACK POCKET!!! Meaning, have an alternative piece ready, because you cannot manage or be evaluated for a poor performance. I don't believe that God honors it. Also, make sure that you have good relationships with college choruses or singers in your area, that are willing to come in and assist. I cannot begin to articulate the number of times I've had to maneuver because of last minute changes in personnel in the chorus. It is what it is, however I hold fast to God's promise, "…He ALWAYS causes me to triumph." And I do!!!

Concise planning for the rehearsal inclusive of proper score analysis, greatly aids in knowing the trouble spots. Sectionals give the proper focus to clarify rhythms and notes. If there are three pieces that need to be reviewed, I would succinctly strategize and allot 10 minutes per selection. It is the reality that choral repertoire takes up the majority of your time, however, it's key to have a strategy. Work smart, not hard. Keep the rehearsal setting vibrant, by working the trouble spots and then connecting the rest. Anytime a chorus starts losing energy, or begins to drift off mentally, without haste I move on to something else. Time is a precious commodity and the conductors job is to get the most done with the time allotted.

The number of pieces allotted for the rehearsal.

Most volunteer church choruses from my experience begin to wane in concentration and performance after 2 hours. Now if I communicate no less than a week in advance, that "I really need an additional 15 minutes the following week," they manage to pull through accordingly. I may give a brief break in between, if I sense the energy level is plummeting. However, I would rather work on three (3) pieces and have thoroughly worked the difficult sections or on to completion, than to rummage through 8 or 9 songs and not accomplish anything in particular.

Energy Level of the Chorus:

For a total goal, I plan for nothing more than a 120 minute rehearsals with my volunteer choir from the church. Now on many levels, we may not necessarily function as a volunteer church Choir, but in actuality that is what and who we are. With that understanding, I have to remind myself that they have committed to offer their personal free time, resources, and mental and emotional gifts to making a difference in the kingdom, and as much as possible I must be sensitive to that. When I sense the energy level shifting, I must be quick to adapt to make the shift to gain the momentum, and sometimes, that's not necessarily a song as it is a brief narrative or as I call it a "fire-side" chat to find out what is going on in the inner workings of the chorus (which most times will not be discovered until I get home and receive that one infamous text message).

VI. What are your expectations in terms of preparation and decorum on the part of chorus members? How do you enforce this?

Clear expectations, terms of preparation, and decorum can be enforced only if clarity of the assignment has been given in ample time. For example, in preparation for our Christmas Concert in December 2014, all scores, practice tapes, uniforms, and a complete rehearsal schedule were disseminated by late August, 2014. There were persons who contacted me in October asking, "What repertoire are you utilizing for Christmas?" I gingerly just respond, "Hmm, I'm working on some exciting repertoire this year…" and quickly, I redirected the conversation elsewhere. It's called, "DO YOUR OWN RESEARCH AND FIND YOUR OWN MUSIC!!" True musicians who are dedicated, do the work!!!!

> THE MORE CONCISE YOU ARE, THE HIGHER THE STANDARD, AND BELIEVE IT OR NOT, THE CHORUS WILL RISE ACCORDINGLY TO THE LEVEL OF YOUR EXPECTATION.

Once I have disseminated needed materials to the chorus, then I can hold them responsible. Within their communication guide it will list repertoire coverage from the first rehearsal upon return from summer recess through the December concert. The more concise you are, the higher the standard, and believe it or not, the chorus will rise accordingly to the level of your expectation.

You have to be clear with the number of rehearsals that are expected to accomplish the task for all involved. As mentioned before, quartets will be utilized at random, to ensure that the repertoire is learned. Let me take a moment to discuss quartet review. Normally I randomly just call names to the front of the rehearsal room to sing a prescribed section, and it is usually a lot of fun, with choir members, trying to assist those on the front-line. However, the goal is not to demean or humiliate anyone, but rather, to send a significant message that it is important to study your music. If there are significant problems, please connect with your section leader or myself for additional help. It is obvious to your fellow choir members, when you've not made attempts. It's not about the quality of the voice, as it is the individual that studies and reviews scores as assigned and is prepared accordingly. Usually the chorus celebrates the weak singers for their bold and accurate attempt.

V. Too many choirs or too few? Is A Young Adult Choir Really essential?

I am amazed when I attend churches that have several adult choirs with significant numbers such as the St. Stephen Baptist of Louisville, Kentucky, the First Baptist Church of Glenarden in Upper Marlboro, Maryland, or the New Psalmist Baptist Church in Baltimore, Maryland, and other significantly larger congregations. These particular congregations warrant the need for a variety of adult, youth, children, and other choral units for the involvement of the vast number of congregants and interests that they have. However, there are those that have followed a prescribed model of Senior Choir no. 1 , Senior Adult Choir no. 2, along with three or four additional groups with unbalanced sections and small numbers. We have to prayerfully assess the relevance, call and purpose of these particular entities. Is there significance in every choral unit displayed? How can we become more relevant, or is that even possible? Are the current participants open to availing themselves to possible change? Has the question been asked, "Why are new members not drawn to this particular ministry or choral unit? What's the overall outlook of the church?

There are so many factors that can prohibit growth and relevance.

Notice I'm staying away from words such as "re-tooling" and "re-inventing." I think it's more about relevancy. I've maintained that my draw to young adults within the primary choral unit at Mississippi Boulevard has been the ability to build relationships with young adults and to strategically involve, utilize and make their presence known while maintaining the security, support and trust of those members who have been a part since the beginning of my tenure. It's a delicate balancing act, however, as I stated, there are unique and strategic ways that have aided in my success:

1. Relevant and current repertoire: I embrace and embody a diverse musical experience for my chorus. That is my purpose and passion, and as I have stated previously, I am emphatically clear about that. On any given Sunday, one might experience, Beethoven's "Hallelujah, (from Mt. Olives), the vibrant and soulful "Worth," by Anthony Brown, to "Yes, God is Real" by the legendary Kenneth Morris. I say that to say, worship for me is an all-encompassing experience that can involve a variety of sacred genres to inspire, edify, set free, and exalt the name of the Lord our God, at the highest caliber. To minimize or negate the fact that all styles of sacred music can be experienced accordingly in worship will cause one to draw an invisible line that separates musical genres, cultures, age, intellect, and spiritual development to a large degree. But God can and will speak through it ALL.

If you are striving to revitalize your chorus, to become

more enticing to young adults, you must be open to the current applications of music repertoire and media usage. To do the same thing and expect different results is not only asinine, but it continues to keep one stifled and irrelevant. I'm intentional about galvanizing all age groups and particularly ensuring that those age groups are out front, replicating the vision with excellence.

2. People are drawn to success. Geoff Colvin, in his book *Innate Talent is Nothing, Success is 99 percent Hard Work,* I couldn't concur with him more. Most of our choruses or entities refuse to put in the work that really makes the difference. It begins not at the level of the rehearsal, but at the prayerful planning and research stages of preparation. I am eternally grateful for both the brilliant teachers and professors who have modelled excellence and stressed the importance of study and training to acquire the rubrics necessary for successful outcomes. I am also eternally grateful for the acknowledgement and deliberate power of God's spirit that rests on my life, which has empowered me to accomplish the tasks given.

It has taken much "deliberate practice" personally and corporately with my chorus to obtain the successes I've encountered. Colvin stresses that *"Deliberate practice is above all an effort of focus and concentration. That is what makes it 'deliberate.'"* We have to be deliberate in our individual and personal research and preparation prior to coming before our choruses, musicians, and praise teams. There's nothing worse than wasting the precious time of fellow "artists" and team members by lack of preparation, which will undoubtedly carry over into the performance.

UNIFORMS

The subject of uniforms is usually a scathing conversation for most choruses. I support the utilization of a committee of men and women to research, present and execute the proper uniform. In addition, I make sure that there are a few plus size persons involved, that I know will make sure that the uniform will look appropriate for all sizes. An in-depth conversation with our choruses about uniforms should be shared as to the sole purpose of biblical expectations of uniforms. The Levitical priests and singers adorned themselves to symbolize the unity within the body. They were no longer individuals as they rendered worship unto God, but they became one. II Chronicles 5:13-14 speaks of when the Ark of the Covenant was brought into the temple. The scripture reflects specifically on the uniformity of the singers and musicians, in apparel and in song. That uniformity of praise rendered unto God, resulted in a response so overwhelmingly experienced by all, "that the priests could not stand to minister because of the cloud, for the glory of the Lord filled the house of God. " (II Chronicles 5:11-14).

Rubrics and expectations can be enforced first, when people really know that the leadership cares about the entire group. Those of us who serve in the capacity of worship pastors, must fully be aware of this call and function in many ways as a pastor.

VI. Transitioning styles of music that minister.

When I arrived at Mississippi Boulevard, there was a solid base of musical appreciation that I had to work with: 1. A talented cadre of singers 2. An appreciation for musical diversity 3. Response to experienced leadership. These were key ingredients that encapsulated my ability to further develop not only my personal gifts, strengths and talents, but to additionally challenge my scholarship and training to seek out more information. Presently, I want to be ever evolving in my gifts and calling. The church has need for more diverse musical excellence, and I'm hopeful that there are those up and coming trained musicians who are answering the call. My prayerful concern is that the African American Church in particular will continue to be an example and provide a place for the trained musician. It's becoming scarce. We will make demands for training in our pulpits but not on our instruments or presiding over our choirs. Additionally, it is of utmost importance that the worship leadership fully understands, and embraces the significance of good sound and audio equipment and personnel. Great equipment and poor technicians will not equal out to a qualitative product. In fact, you frustrate your paid music staff members and volunteer worship participants, who prepare for a qualitative presentation but they cannot hear, or the sound is distorted, etc.

I've had the pleasure of working with one of the finest sound and audio engineers for several years at Mississippi Boulevard. I've asked Mr. Jonathan Cross to submit what he deems as essential for qualitative sound and audio equipment.

Sound Doctrine, Sound Teaching, & the Sound System

By Mr. Jonathan Cross
President & Chief of System Design, BCS, Inc: Better Concert, Church, & Community Sound, Inc.;
Director of Media & Chief Audio Engineer, Mississippi Blvd. Christian Church

The visionary modern church will thrive when it is based on a foundation of sound doctrine, when its pastors and teachers faithfully communicate that doctrine through sound teaching that is clear and concise, and when the people can hear, worship, and engage fully in spirit and in truth, while experiencing the word and well-rehearsed music and song; while listening to a high quality artifact-free sound system that is well-adjusted and expertly operated.

Sound is to be seen, not heard. Meaning that when the sound and audio is good, people should say the music was excellent, and the preaching impactful, not that something was too loud, or indiscernible. Thus, they may see the speakers and equipment hanging, but they should not hear artifacts like feedback, buzzes, tonal anomalies, and/or excessive loudness. Yet, because the worship environment is also an emotional one, the experience must be one in which the audio not only sounds good, but feels good. Therefore, the mantra for the modern church's chief audio engineer must be to 1) Protect the System; 2) Protect Ears, 3) Make it Sound Good, and 4) Make it Feel Good. When these four tenets are committed to and achieved, then sound will be seen and not heard, and services will be artifact free. In order to have a successful audio experience in church, the modern church needs to commit to the following 7 things:

1. Invest Wisely

The visionary church must have pastoral and spiritual leadership committed to empowering the music and production ministries to go before the people with excellence. This means they are unencumbered by substandard and unreliable equipment. In order to ensure the success and growth of the ministry, the church must proactively make quality investments in the 1) Audio and Media Systems, 2) the Acoustic Treatment of the sanctuary and Worship Spaces, and 3) the Engineering Staff and their auxiliary media team support. These investments MUST be made 1) Early On; 2) On an Ongoing Basis; and 3) Proactively as periodic strategic equipment upgrades every 10-15 years.

Invest in PROPER System Design. This must be done patiently and thoroughly. Invest in design in the very early stages of any building or expansion project. Audio should not be an afterthought, or be regulated to last minute budget allocations. The audio system is the #1 point of contact for worshippers and guests at your church. EVERYTHING is done and performed through the sound system. The music, and the sermon are your key emotional catalysts, and the system must not get in the way of conveying them both. The hours of prayer, of sermon study and writing, and the weeks of musical rehearsals must not be held back by the system. Thus, in any facility purchase, construction, expansion, or upgrade, the Audio system Must be your Number ONE budget priority. You get one chance to get it right. You can always re-paint, re-carpet, or re-upholster, but it is VERY costly to upgrade a poorly installed system, or a system installed as an afterthought. The time to both have the greatest impact, as well as maximize the bang for the buck invested in the church's audio, is early on.

Avoid purchasing equipment just because you saw it at another church. Their solution may not be the best solution for you. This is where patient design and research will pay off, as well as having a quality hiring process, such that the church leadership can have the utmost confidence in the recommendations and opinions of the Chief Audio Engineer. Go with the right solution for your house of worship, not what works for someone else.

Three caveats:

1) ALWAYS design and build extra capacity into your systems. Your ministry and your audio needs will grow, and it is much more cost effective to build capacity in at the beginning. This is guaranteed. And;

2) For key components, specifically the Main and Monitor Mixing Console, DO purchase and install a recognized INDUSTRY Standard live sound console. This will ensure that your facilities are also able to function as turn-key performance and worship venues. Visiting artists and engineers will be able to easily adjust to and perform on the system. Also, reliability and quick acute exchange of parts will be pretty much guaranteed during the life of the venue and equipment. Standardize your consoles across multi-site ministry campuses, as well as within the various venues within any main campus.

3) Invest in professionally designed acoustic treatment for your actual worship space. A million dollar PA system in an untreated space is a negligence that will undermine the system, as well as yield dismal audio results, thus leading to a constant barrage of complaints by leaders and parishioners alike. Like the system itself, the investment in the actual sound of the acoustic space is of paramount importance.

2. Hire Right & Empower Your Team

Procure highly knowledgeable and skilled engineers. Establish and maintain a high standard for the audio expectation, yet be careful not to micromanage your engineers. Instead, hire right, so that you may have complete confidence in your engineering team/staff.

Choose the right engineers. Hire right by interviewing right. The interviewing and selection process is key. Make sure that experienced engineers are part of your hiring process, as no one on the church staff (who is not an engineer, or who does not have substantial experience working very closely with live and recording engineers) will know the right questions to ask, or the right queries to make. As such, the candidate that looks good on paper could know absolutely nothing of practical use. This is especially true of graduates of audio recording programs. They may have lots of classroom instruction, but very little high pressure in-the-field experience, nor may they have enjoyed having been mentored over a quality time period such that they learn and gain pertinent incites that can be the difference between quality sound and an un-damaged PA system that may cost the church tens of thousands of dollars in repair costs over a very short time frame.

3. Celebrate Your Audio People:

When the sound is absolutely on point, the audio engineer generally receives no notice or accolade. Instead, what is generally stated is "The music was great today, etcetera..." However, when there is any semblance of a problem, whether it is actually caused by the engineer(s) or not, the people literally turn and look at the engineer, and say something to the effect of "What are they doing up there? Etcetera..." In other words, engineers receive hardly any of the accolades, but much of the blame. Yet, unlike the musicians, singers, and even the pastor, the engineering staff doesn't get to practice for the day's or event's services or performances. Instead, the engineer must accept what happens immediately on the spot. There are no do-overs, and no subsequent notes or chords to cover up bad notes, missed cues, or misspoken words or stumbled on texts. But, the engineers can have 2-3000 pairs of ears all formulating an opinion about the one and done mixing performance. So, when things go well and without a hitch, be sure to openly celebrate the success and performance of the engineer and media staff. This will go a long way, and will render immeasurable performance results in the future.

4. Control Stage Volume:
Empower the church's engineers to have authority and control over the overall level of volume emanating from the stage and pulpit areas. Excessive Stage volume has the tendency to smear the intelligibility of sound from the main front of the house speaker system. Thus, it must be managed and controlled aggressively.

5. Train Pastors, Singers, and Musicians:
Train your worship participants on the proper techniques for using, holding, and speaking into microphones, as well as approaching monitor speakers, and using mics around monitors. Both Pastors and Singers would do well to know that the engineer cannot electronically make their speech, singing, or preaching louder beyond a certain point without introducing feedback into the system and environment. Thus, preacher and singers must know that their role is to EXCITE THE MIC. Literally. They must enunciate and project their voices at all times.

6. Empower:
When the church has gone through the proper process to hire right, then EMPOWER your production team and engineers such that they are EQUAL PARTNERS with the churches musical production team. This

keeps pertinent parties on equal footing such that no one is positioned to undermine another, or undermine important technical decisions that protect the system, protect ears, make it sound good, and make it feel good. This approach produces and fosters MUTUAL Respect, Cooperation, and Harmony between the technical and musical teams for the absolute good of the church.

Listen: Listen to your engineer, both his/her opinions about the sound, AND the actual sound that they achieve. If there emerges a lack of confidence in the technical opinions of the engineer, then do not belabor the matter. Replace the engineer. Whomever is the engineer must be trusted, as the role itself is one where the engineer must use his/her professional judgment to render opinions about the sound. No one can hear inside of the engineer's head. So, either they get it right or they don't, according to the standards established previously. If differences of opinion become a pervasively persistent matter, then a change is in order.

QUESTIONS FOR INTROSPECTION/
SMALL GROUP DISCUSSION

❶ What is your personal philosophy of music ministry? How does your personal philosophy tie into the goals and branding of the assignment you've called too?

❷ Is there a clear cut approach or methodology as it pertains to the hiring of competent staff members? What evaluation tool is used? How often? Monthly, Quarterly. Annually?

❸ Are choral units functioning at the optimal level (i.e. spiritually, musically, numerically)? Are there too many choirs? Is there a contention between choirs and leadership that deflects from honoring God?

❹ How are you discerning the appropriate repertoire or musical appetite for the music ministry and congregation? What gauge or evaluation tool helps assess what is meeting the needs, challenging and edifying?

❺ If a musical director is on your staff, does he/she envelop fully the message of "team" with voice and instrument? Is there a sense of genuine camaraderie or competition?

CHAPTER 6
Excellence: *PLANNING FOR WEEKLY SUCCESS:*
(Planning, Possessing, Prepping, with Power and Passion)

T he role of the leader of Pastoral Worship is to *allow the Scriptures to shape a series of individual expressions that, in their totality, will enable the worship community to experience a unified event. Liturgy is the totality of what happens verbally and nonverbally when the people of God find themselves in dialogue with the triune God who initiates the conversation and seeks to become enfleshed in the event of Word and Sacrament.* These basic tenets are the essential components necessary for successful and consistent planning. The summation of worship, I believe, is the interconnectedness of every component working together to experience the glory and the power of God.

Below are significant components that must be a part of the many stages of planning and preparing for a powerful and passionate worship service, and other designated sacred music events:

Team Building:
As the Pastor of worship, do team members trust that you have their backs? How are you formulating relationships with your team? Are you fully supportive of their dreams as per their assignments? Are they keeping in line with the overall vision of the church? There are all kinds of issues, problems, remedies, suggestions, etc. when it comes to building and maintaining a sacred team. One of the greatest pressures of serving in the capacity as a worship leader is that of "weekly evaluation." Those

of us who serve are on the front line each and every week (especially those who have considerably credible ministries), the expectation from the congregation is extremely HIGH.

For this reason, I try to keep an "open door" policy with all staff members at all times. They know they can call my personal cell, email, set up conference calls etc., when and as needed. However, I hold them accountable to their tasks and vice versa. The expectation as mentioned earlier is "high performance," and I don't settle for anything less. Honestly, there have been lots of transitions with not only the worship ministry staff but in general at my current place of tenure. Some transitions have been warranted; others were due to bad hires, and some just knew it was time to move onto the next assignment. It's all been a tremendous learning experience in the following areas: 1. Prayerful discernment 2. Skillset assessment 3. DNA fit for the vision of the church and the team. In addition, I want to take a moment to talk about personal integrity and character as a leader. First, I'm not at all in the cadre of individuals who deem themselves flawless and perfect, however I do strongly believe in the importance of maintaining integrity within the context of our leadership positions. I have learned the importance of accountability partnerships. There are those who hold me accountable on different levels. I have personal accountability partner(s), who can ask anything they desire to ask, or sense, if I'm shifting off track. I also have accountability "career" partners, with whom I communicate on a weekly basis. These are the people that I share the weights and stresses of ministry. On every level, I have the full assurance that my honesty is secure and will not be utilized against me for self-aggrandizement purposes. More importantly and in addition to established accountability, the greatest weapon to ensure success for a life filled with integrity and character is my daily fellowship with the Lord, Jesus Christ. I have learned the importance of being established fully in God's word and knowing that I am the "righteousness of God by faith in Christ Jesus." God is not looking at us as it relates to our proclivities or sin. His concern is that He sees His son, Jesus Christ, living fully in our lives. I no longer walk in the condemnation of error, but in the victory of His Son living and abiding in my life. With that in mind, I'm not flawless, but I'm walking a more victorious life than I ever have before. *praisebreak*

So it's important that we model before our staff members, a life akin to that of a saint. Walking with integrity is priceless. It serves as a premiere model for team members. If we err, then being big enough to offer an apology (by saying the words openly that "I WAS WRONG. PLEASE FORGIVE ME) is important. What a powerful display! I've had to learn to identify and accept the responsibility of my wrongdoings. When I didn't accept full responsibility, the resentment and outcome were not in the best interest for myself or the team. Now, I try my best to live in the prism of a resounding theme given to me by my former pastor, Dr. Frank Anthony Thomas, "Do the right thing in all relationships." No other way about it!!!

Formulating relationships with team/staff members takes time. I firmly believe that solid relationships are built on the following foundational pillars: clear expectations (job descriptions), accountability, follow-through, honest communication, and loving support.

The 21st Century Industry Band? How can you handle such talent in one setting?
Over the last 26 years, I've been fortunate enough to work with the finest cadre of instrumentalists ever. Yet, it's taken hard intentional

personal and corporate work to mesh our personalities, and to ascertain a mutual respect for each other's gifts and talents, while at the same time functioning out of my own ability to deal honestly with whatever insecurities that might surface. In addition, dealing with the plight of disconcerting realities from others with hidden agendas can be onerous. Why? Because their ultimate goal is not to be right, but to divide and completely undermine my personal standard and corporate vision.

The "21st Century Industry Band", is a title that I prefer to use for this publication in order to describe those individuals who not only bring a wide range of skill, musical diversity and experience, but in addition, often accompany or serve as musical directors for premiere sacred or secular artists. These persons serve in their own right as producers, musical directors for major artists, and overall, they are just accomplished musicians in their own right. Depending on the church budget, resources, talent pool, etc. if you are able to hire competent, reliable staff members, I strongly recommend that you research and interview carefully. First, after verifying via the interview process the talent of the interviewee and the decision or general consensus is confirmed, make sure that you are clear about your expectations. Having clarity in the area of expectations is essential. Below is a general job description that I utilize, as you will note it clearly specifies the following:

Job Title
Principle Function
Job Duties
Minimum Requirements
Signature of Employee
Signature of Employer

Clarity is a non-negotiable for me. Everyone is much easier to hold accountable upon full knowledge, awareness and acceptance of their responsibilities and expectations.

Preparing Musicians:
Finding the right synergy for your team, church and overall ministry is essential. I have heard many fine choirs with very poor musicians accompanying them, or vice versa. Thankfully, we've been blessed essentially with a steady quality of both. The expectation is extremely high and there are those that just cannot meet the criteria, or the high expectation, and that is understandable.

It takes a considerable amount of time and team-building to have a viable team, to not only execute, but to function in other capacities as needed. As I reflect, there have been 6 strong musical directors that I can readily identify over my tenure. Let me chronologically identify:

1992-1994 (Anthony Walker)
1995-1997 (Jason Clark)
1997-1999 (Pamela Jean Davis)
2000-2010 (Roderick Vester)
2010-2013   (Kenneth Hollins)
2013-present (A. Christopher Morris)

Each have identifiable leadership patterns and styles as musical directors, and each brought a unique flavor to the overall team. However the rubric and expectation was one of fully being prepared and executing with excellence and the power of God. I've learned how to somewhat re-tool myself with each team, which tends to always be significantly younger than me as the years progress. Lets say it's been a give and take. But interestingly enough, most staff members are forewarned about the no non-sense policies at the Blvd., prior to even applying for a position.

1. No late arrivals for rehearsals and services (Non-excused or repetitive habits)
2. Shirt and Tie policy for Sunday morning worship services (unless otherwise advised)
3. Thorough knowledge of repertoire assignments.

Those are the essential criteria outlined as well as other expectations. We have a very strong bond, respect and appreciation for each other. It's a team that I would guarantee against any, and I thank God for their gifts and the relationships. We do a pretty good job of holding one another accountable when necessary, and hearing one another out as necessary.

As I stated earlier, the expectation for musical excellence is high. That is not to say that this expectation overrides our humanness to respect one another and to love each other. I've learned through some harsh decisions, everything cannot be done directly "by the book" as I've learned never to allow talent to hold me hostage. It's a balancing act that only gets better as we trust and learn to build our personal relationships with each other and Jesus Christ.

I have interviewed several persons below who have functioned at one time as a Musical Director for a church or with a premier gospel artist. Five (5) questions have been posed for each to share their views as it relates to the approach for a successful ensemble with staff musicians of varying levels of expertise:

1. What are the essential steps/processes for creating a "good to great" church band/instrumental ensemble?

2. What tactics do you utilize to accomplish a "unified" ensemble?

3. How do you go about establishing a unit that serves as accompaniment to varying assigned age church choirs (i.e. children, youth, young adult, adult, senior)?

4. What would you deem important qualifications for a music director at a church of any size?

5. How do you measure weekly successes?

Natalie Ragins
(Keyboardist/Organist, currently on tour w/Tyler Perry's stage play,
"Madea On The Run." Atlanta, GA.)

1. What are the essential steps/processes for creating a "good to great" church band/instrumental ensemble?
I believe that the band mates should possess "like mindedness."
This doesn't mean they should be clones. The musicians should
have very similar goals, as it relates to the ministry: 1. A heart
for God. 2. A heart for the ministry. 3. Availability and dedication
4. Flexibility.

2. What tactics do you utilize to accomplish a "unified" ensemble?
I'd basically implement the previously mentioned qualities.
Musicians tend to be very cooperative when they feel
appreciated, loved, and a genuine sincerity from his/her leader.
Basically, it's the same principle in real life: people will go
above and beyond when they feel loved and appreciated.

3. How do you go about establishing a unit that serves as accompaniment to varying assigned age church choirs (i.e. children, youth, young adult, adult, senior)?
Basically, I search for a unit that's versatile in various styles, as
well as willing to learn and implement new ideas/approaches. It
all goes back to the first response. As a leader, it's my duty to
be upfront with my staff and to prepare them for the task at hand.

It starts with our initial introduction/meeting. They should be aware of what the job entails, prior to accepting.

4. What would you deem important qualifications for a music director at a church of any size?

Obviously, he/she should be highly skilled in the area. I also believe that a Musical Director should have a heart for God, the Pastor, the church, people, and a gift to lead the people.

5. How do you measure weekly successes?

Weekly successes, to me, are relative to the overall requirements... which are based on the vision of the house. Maintaining the musical/professional expectations are key. Everyone should be held (musically/professionally) accountable.

Trent Phillips

(Lionheart Music, Inc. Music Production/Media/Consulting-Atlanta, GA.)

1. What are the essential steps/processes for creating a "good to great" church band/instrumental ensemble?

Vision must be caught. I'm a firm believer in putting the vision before people and challenging them to reach for it. If your band is not currently performing up to their highest potential, communicate your vision first. Let them know clearly the areas in which they need to improve. Challenge their individual practice regimen to go to another level. Lengthen band rehearsal time where needed. Establish some form of consequence when the music is not executed effectively. Above all else: Inspire them. Encourage them. Believe in them!

2. What tactics do you utilize to accomplish a "unified" ensemble?

Prayer: *Keep the focus Christ-Centered! Communication: Talk about everything that matters.*

Practice: *Cohesion is built through time spent in rehearsals and listening to each other. Study Others: As a group, go check out other church bands that are doing things big! Fellowship: Encourage the bandmates to enjoy fellowship time outside of rehearsals and services.*

3. How do you go about establishing a unit that serves as accompaniment to varying assigned age church choirs (i.e. children, youth, young adult, adult, senior)?

The most important factor here is staffing well-rounded musicians who can execute various styles of music with authenticity according to the choir's repertoire. Many larger churches assign lead musicians (often keyboardists) from their band staff to handle music for their choirs by age group or style. Staff wisely!

4. What would you deem important qualifications for a music director at a church of any size?

1. Be skilled on a lead instrument with at least 10 years of playing experience. 2. Play in all keys well. 3. Know intermediate to advance musical theory. 4. Be able to read music. 5. Be well balanced. Know various church hymns, gospel/worship songs (classic to contemporary) 6. Be able to play with other musicians well. 7. Have integrity, great accountability, good interpersonal and communication skills and be respectful of leadership.

5. How do you measure weekly successes?

Professionalism (Timelines, Accountability, etc.), Musical Preparedness and Execution, Proper Decorum and Uniform; Spirituality: Was the atmosphere/feel of the room (audience) noticeably affected by the musicians' contribution to the worship service?

Roy J. Cotton, II
(CEO, songFLO.com Desoto, Texas)

1. What are the essential steps/processes for creating a "good to great" church band/instrumental ensemble?
Assessing everyone's skill sets to ensure that everyone is equally yoked on a skill level. Know everyone's background. Secondly, understand personality traits to discover who is the band leader. Thirdly, develop a sustainable process for practicing and rehearsing in preparation for performance.

2. What tactics do you utilize to accomplish a "unified" ensemble?
Everyone must foster a personal relationship outside of music to develop a unified ensemble. Most of our band problems exist because musicians don't understand one another on a personal level. When one discovers another's upbringing, family history, etc. it helps him or her to communicate better.

3. How do you go about establishing a unit that serves as accompaniment to varying assigned age church choirs (i.e. children, youth, young adult, adult, senior)?
Encourage the 'listening' aspect of music ministry so that musicians can respect all genres. The secret is to keep the performance value of every song at a professional level. Many praise and worship songs have well-produced band arrangements, but hymns aren't recorded at the same level. It is very important that musicians are given time to develop older songs at the same level of the new ones.

4. What would you deem important qualifications for a music director at a church of any size?

1. Love God and His people

2. Have a heart for ministry

3. Have a theological understanding and a teaching ability to lead the music ministry.

4. Know how to use or delegate planning center online.

5. Know how to use or delegate Pro Presenter

6. Know how to use stems and multitracks

7. Know how to sight read hymns straight out of the hymnal

8. Know how to administer and fully accompany the variety of sacred music styles (i.e. from praise and worship, choral selections, and solo works.)

5. How do you measure weekly successes?

If the music ministry presented was authentic (not perfect) then we should be able to see a glimpse of what God will do in service by how he moved through us during the week. Did we practice at home before rehearsal? Did we arrive at rehearsal on time? Did we know the music well enough to improvise together on Sunday morning? These questions determine our effectiveness.

Tyries Rolf

(Music Director, First Baptist Church Broad, Memphis, TN.)

1. What are the essential steps/processes for creating a "good to great" church band/instrumental ensemble?

It begins with core leadership. From a personal standpoint, my music director must possess the necessary skills to be able to handle multiple attitudes, as well as the ability to lead effectively. Spiritually, each musician must know his/her role as it pertains to the worship service. They should 1. Understand how to play as a BAND effectively 2. Understand how to be efficient in worship. 3. Pay attention to worship shifts 4. Not miss key 'moments' to help carry the service.

2. What tactics do you utilize to accomplish a "unified" ensemble?

It first starts with relationship. I always let my musicians know I support them. Especially if they are performing at a high level weekly. Sometimes we become so **TO TRULY BE UNIFIED, YOU HAVE TO BE CONNECTED.** *production-oriented and so focused on presentation, that we forget we are dealing with human beings with different upbringings and different circumstances. To truly be unified, you have to be connected.*

3. How do you go about establishing a unit that serves as accompaniment to varying assigned age church choirs (i.e. children, youth, young adult, adult, senior)?

My particular age range for my staff is 22-47. Each person in their own respective way is connected to their era musically. Being so, we have a vast majority of styles to be able to pull from, as well as having an actual person from that era to effectively give their perspective.

4. What would you deem important qualifications for a music director at a church of any size?

1. Relationship with God. I would dare not have someone in a leadership role who wasn't able to effectively pray or lead spiritually. 2. Experience- whether church experience in the past or experience in the music industry. 3. Skill- from hymnals to contemporary songs, I would want him to execute both. 4. Problem Solver - He/She must have the necessary patience/understanding to deal with everything that comes along with the position.

5. How do you measure weekly successes?

My weekly success is measured by a few things: 1. How well was the music ministry received by the congregation? 2. Did we create an atmosphere conducive to the worship experience? 3. Did we help or hinder the Pastor or speaker in His/Her delivery of the message? 4. Were souls encouraged to come and the body of Christ edified?

Anthony Walker
(Music Director-LEDISI, Bowie, MD.)

1. What are the essential steps/processes for creating a "good to great" church band/instrumental ensemble?

I believe the essential process for creating a great band, church or "otherwise" is skillful flexibility. They must have a large well of musical styles as resources. Jazz, classical, traditional and contemporary gospel styles, everything in between (hip-hop, neo soul) as well as a working knowledge of modern technology. Today's players have the ability to learn music very fast and have strong improvisational skills. There must be a team concept, much like a basketball or football team. Everyone in their respective lane. That's just the rhythm section.

2. What tactics do you utilize to accomplish a "unified" ensemble?

One, have clear expectations of what's required to serve in this capacity. Two, make sure the players have enough time to learn the music required. Three (but really first), pray together and study. Four, make sure they are submitted to the established authority. whether it's the Pastor, Worship Pastor, Music Director, The Artist featured, etc. Five, periodic fellowship times away from the church building. (Restaurants, Movies, Bowling, etc.)

3. How do you go about establishing a unit that serves as accompaniment to varying assigned age church choirs (i.e. children, youth, young adult, adult, senior)?

Although one would think that age appropriate musicians should match the unit they're playing for, it's not always possible because of skill, maturity level, and budget. Instead, if you have a versatile rhythm section that's able to play multiple styles, it's possible to move the pianist, organist, etc. in and out of the lead musician chair to whatever ensemble is ministering.

4. What would you deem important qualifications for a music director at a church of any size?

1. Must be saved with a demonstrated walk with Jesus Christ. 2. A serious student of the bible and its principles. 3. An expert on their main instrument and/or vocal production. 4. Higher Education, preferably in music but not required but, a degree in a related field is most desirable 5. Works exceptionally well with people. 6. Submitted to the vision of the pastor/church 7. Strong communication skills. 8. Preferably a music reader. 9. Keeps up with modern technologies as they are pivotal in today's music offerings.

5. How do you measure weekly successes?

First and foremost, if there's an abiding sense of the presence of God where you are able to tell the Congregation's reception of the musical presentation. Further if there are unsaved people at the service who come forward for salvation, it's a great day. On a purely musical basis, if the execution of a challenging work (i.e., skilled and reputable anthem or spiritual) is done to the point where the congregation is visibly moved and blessed, it's considered a great day.

John Stoddart

(Music Director (Kirk Whalum), Songwriter, Producer, and Recording Artist, Huntsville, AL)

1. What are the essential steps/processes for creating a "good to great" church band/instrumental ensemble?

A few years ago, I had the privilege of participating in a Christmas TV special that was filmed at a large church in Houston. I arrived during a lull in the rehearsal but immediately took note of the sheer number of musicians on stage. There was a full orchestra, choir, drums, bass, guitar, TWO keyboardists PLUS organ and soloists! My initial thought was, "this is going to be a mess" because, in my experience to that point, the number of musicians was directly proportionate to the amount of chaos on the stage. Fortunately, I was delightfully mistaken. The ensemble was wonderful! There was great balance between the singers, rhythm section and orchestra. The rhythm players were disciplined and humble and the entire production was held together and directed by a competent minister of music and musical director. It was one of the most comprehensive displays I have ever seen of the critical elements necessary for a great instrumental ensemble to be effective. Here are a few principles on which to build a successful musical ensemble.

THE FIRST STEP IN CREATING YOUR DESIRED CULTURE IS TO IDENTIFY A LEADER THAT EMBODIES THE CHARACTERISTICS YOU WANT TO INSTILL.

Leadership - *Culture reflects leadership. The first step in creating your desired culture is to identify a leader that embodies the characteristics you want to instill. You will find a Godly, organized, knowledgeable, decisive and self-assured person at the head of any successful church music ensemble. It will be virtually impossible to apply any of the other principles until this one is addressed.*

Vision *-Musicians are, by design, creative. There is almost no limit to the number of ideas you could generate and develop just within your own musical group. Many ensembles lack cohesion and effectiveness because the vision for the musical culture of the church (or event) was never established. The musical-cultural goals and objectives for the church are prayerfully developed by the pastor(s) and the minister of music. The minister of music then selects one or more musical directors to execute that vision.*

Communication *-Vision is only effective when it is effectively communicated. I served as pipe organist at an historic African American Baptist church in Washington, DC that utilized traditional hymns as well as contemporary Gospel throughout the service. The music director set clear boundaries and directives regarding roles for each style. So each musician knew that, for example, the pipe organ would lead the morning hymn, the bass guitar and Hammond B3 should tacit and the drums would only play cymbal swells going into and during the last verse. The choral meditational selection before the sermon, however, would be led from the piano. It would include the rhythm section and* *the pipe organ would be tacit. The B3 was to fill the "space" to facilitate the transition between that movement and the preaching moment. Clear communication about the vision, the culture and my role eliminated any confusion.*

__Synergy Leadership,__ vision and communication form the foundation on which synergy can grow and thrive.

One of my greatest joys is working as the musical director for a Grammy Award winning Jazz saxophonist. It's a 5-piece band that has traveled the world together from Tokyo to Johannesburg.

SYNERGY WITHOUT BOUNDARIES CAN QUICKLY DEVOLVE INTO CHAOS.

While we've always enjoyed making music together, the synergy and freedom we have after almost 10 years together far surpasses that of the first year. Even our families have gotten to know each other and it's had an undeniable impact on the music we create together.

__Discipline__ Synergy without boundaries can quickly devolve into chaos. Going back to the example of the TV Christmas special, there was one thing that, to this day, still stands out in my mind. The organist/3rd keyboardist only played 2 or 3 notes about every 8 bars for the entire evening. He exercised great musical restraint and discipline in filling a role that was critical to the ensemble's success that night. Playing any more than he did would have detracted from the overall presentation. Lesson: you're part of a team and every part is important, no matter how small. See 1st Corinthians 12:12.

Anointing

Have you ever purchased a new song or CD and listened to it all day everyday for 2 weeks? You were just blown away by the singing or musicianship but the impact sort of wore off after a while. Then there's that song that, even after 10 years, still brings you to tears just like the first time you heard it. That's the difference between talent and anointing. Talent can "wow" you but only the Anointing can touch you! The calling of a musician is a high one that involves a lifetime of work and the development of gifts and talents. But we must never lose sight of the fact that our only real power for affecting someone's heart comes from the anointing of the Spirit of God.

TALENT CAN "WOW" YOU BUT ONLY THE ANOINTING CAN TOUCH YOU!

Steven Ford, M.A.

(Professor of Music, Eastern University St. David, Pennsylvania)

1. What are the essential steps/processes for creating a "good to great" church band/instrumental ensemble?

When creating a good ensemble, it is proper to choose individuals with exceptional musical ability, however, when I reflect on the process of creating a "Great Instrumental Ensemble" I've found it necessary to demand much more. My process has been established on the word "comp" from a jazz literary perspective. "To comp" in the jazz world identifies the musician who is responsible to accompany the soloist. He or she must provide the chord changes and the textured harmonies, which allows the lead player the support and freedom to present their ideas, motif development and expression without creative collision, and unprecedented support.

With this paradigm in mind, I look for individuals who not only reverence God and display an exemplar of a righteous lifestyle, but also one who possesses the highest level of musicianship, the ability to be a team player, willing to shine in the shadow of others, equipped to harmonize with others musically, morally and spiritually, understand and demonstrate humility, level headedness in business, dependable, a consistent ability to follow directives, be cognizant of and be subservient to leadership. If and when an individual demonstrates all of the above, I am confident that their inclusion will always "comp" or compliment and prove beneficial to the success of any music and fine arts department.

2. What would you deem important qualifications for a music director at a church of any size?

When lecturing about leadership I teach my "d+d = s" principle, which stands for, "Direction plus Delivery, equates to Success." In short, the success of the music and fine arts program simply means that the music director must always deliver. He or she must be able to deliver a consistent and effective musical and creative repertoire that is diverse and embraced by your demographic audience. Be connected to your senior pastor, and learn their likes and dislikes. Be connected to your department, and learn your team as well as the opposition within your team, (those who oppose you are planted there for your development, so learn how to embrace them, they will refine your leadership abilities, ... trust me, I know from personal experience!)

You must develop the qualities necessary to understand submission to Godly leadership, senior leadership, humility, administration, responsibility, accountability, organization, musical skill, excellence, punctuality, and spirituality. Additionally, it is essential that you develop, maintain and deliver a consistent life of prayer, Bible study as well as an ongoing commitment to enhancing your musical pedagogy. Lastly, the growth and the sustaining power of healthy census in regard to membership of any church, is uniquely connected to the weekly presentation of the music and arts department. The reality of that principle is not only determined by the presentation and sermons of the senior pastor, but it is also crucial with respect to the consistency of the musical director, who must always deliver, in excellence.

Pamela Jean Davis

(Worship Arts Director, Fountain of Praise Church, Houston TX)

1. What are the essential steps/processes for creating a "good to great" church band/instrumental ensemble?

Appreciate one another's gift, talent and or skill. Allow musicians to be open and share their inner thoughts musically. The Pastor must engage with the church band by feeding the vision of the church and sow in personal time with the band a few times a year. The unit must also be teachable, reachable and trainable. It is vital who we allow to accompany and create music for God's worship services. Build up positive thinkers and believers. This will keep you motivated with support, knowing your placement and calling is not in vain.

2. What tactics do you utilize to accomplish a "unified" ensemble?

A job description including duties as assigned. Clarity on pay scale and raises by holding them accountable to their word. Give the unit air to breathe without lingering over their shoulder. Build trust by respecting their gift. Outside fellowships away from paid environment. Mindfully keep the unit aware by demonstrating and illustrating a less talented unit but have all the other pieces, character, heart, integrity and love for God and people. Open the door for the ensemble to figure out the solution from time to time. You may have the answer, but give them the opportunity to feel important, wanted and needed.

3. How do you go about establishing a unit that serves as an accompaniment to varying assigned age church choirs (i.e. children, youth, young adult, adult, senior)?

Locate the right size glove to fit the hand for all components. Create a unit that will best compliment the age, church and choirs. Occasionally we must give the assigned age groups what they ask for to fulfill their appetite, but the Director holds the cards. Always have a spiritual and musical hand that is trainable and able to support the complete body. While establishing a unit that serves, have a good map/vision for the future.

4. What would you deem important qualifications for a music director at a church of any size?

Understand the vision of the church. Be prepared. Training in your profession, along with technique, helps to educate the church when you have been exposed to other genres of music. You are the engine of the music ministry. Build a team that speaks the same language or other languages to broaden the music ministry. You must have all parts in good working condition to produce music and shift effectively. The church music ministry will always reflect the music director and Pastor. Be willing to learn more, do more and share more.

5. How do you measure weekly successes?

I measure weekly successes by learning to disconnect myself with work overload. Praying, planning and preparing a thoughtful process that works best for me includes a team of corporate assistance. Becoming wiser forces my intelligence to creatively prioritize. This state of mind allows time to exhale away from the bondage of restraints that weigh me down. I must stop, be silent, listen and move in the turning flow of the Spirit. Being a risk taker leads me more into becoming a stronger faith walker in the Lord. With these measures, the outcome becomes God's success.

Roderick Vester, M.A., M.M.
(Minister of Music, First Baptist Church-Broad, Memphis, TN)

1. What are the essential steps/processes for creating a "good to great" church band/instrumental ensemble?

While there are a myriad of steps for creating a good to great church band, I believe most can be compiled into three concepts: Passion, Motivation, and Action. Each band member must find their element and channel all of their energies (thoughts and feelings) toward that one thing, thus becoming a driven force of one that is unstoppable. Motivation helps one become a driven individual. Action is necessary to move a church ensemble from good to great. When these three concepts are realized, healthy synergy occurs and helps propels the entire ensemble to greatness.

2. What tactics do you utilize to accomplish a "unified" ensemble?

A unified ensemble occurs before it is formed. Personality types, strength and growth areas of each individual, temperaments, and emotional maturity are all important things to explore upon the creation of an ensemble. Only when these traits are thoroughly examined can a unified ensemble take shape. Next, vision, mission, and strategy must be communicated clearly by the leader to the ensemble. Trust must be built between all parties. Acceptance of one another is crucial to creating a safe environment where ideas can be shared and respected. Lastly, healthy dissent should be fostered for this helps with the concept of alignment.

3.How do you go about establishing a unit that serves as an accompaniment to varying assigned age church choirs (i.e. *children, youth, young adult, adult, senior)?*

The style of music within each age specific church choir should dictate how to recruit or hire this ensemble. Recruiting in house would be a great place to start. There are often retired skilled musicians within the congregation that are eager to serve if asked. Establishing an age0specific ensemble should also be considered because beyond musical capability, one must examine social, emotional, cultural, and developmental issues.

4. What would you deem important qualifications for a music director at a church of any size?

A heart and desire to serve is the most important qualification for a music director at a church of any size. Success and longevity in church ministry directly depends on acceptance and support, which is difficult to earn without genuine love for people and passion for the work. Honed technical and performance skills are critical - along with humility, dedication, leadership, punctuality, discipline (in and outside of the church), a positive attitude, a diverse repertoire, and a placid temperament. The ability to engage with non-musicians in the church is also imperative for success because all persons must work together for the overall success of the ministry.

5. How do you measure weekly successes?

I measure weekly success based on performance goals for each particular week, which are an extension of the rehearsal objectives for that same week. Some questions I ask are: Was the music executed as expected and as outlined on the performance goals sheet? Was there a successful transfer of musicality from the rehearsal room to the stage? Were technical issues truly resolved in the rehearsal room or did they re-surface on stage? If so, where did I fail in the process of teaching? Ultimately, the true measure of success is whether people were inspired, influenced, encouraged, educated, and empowered by the musical presentation.

Cedric Thompson
(Producer, Engineer, Instrumentalist – Charlotte, NC)

1. What are the essential steps/processes for creating a "good to great" church band/instrumental ensemble?

First I think that knowing where you are in terms of the atmosphere of the church (vision of the pastor concerning church and music) needs to be identified. From there you can put a band or ensemble together. Secondly, making sure that the members of the band/ ensemble have great chemistry and that each member understands each other's roles. Thirdly, make sure that individuals represent great character (they don't have to be the greatest player around the area but they should be able to be effective on their instrument).

2.What tactics do you utilize to accomplish a "unified" ensemble?

Make sure you choose individuals who respect not only each other but the music that they have to play. It would be good also to have someone who can play more than one instrument. Having designated rehearsals separate from the singers even if it is 1-2 hours before the singers rehearse with the band. Make sure everyone is aware of the music by providing music to them maybe a week ahead or at least a few days ahead either via some type of planning center or some type of created inbox where they can get the music that is planned for the week.

3. How do you go about establishing a unit that serves as an accompaniment to varying assigned age church choirs (i.e. children, youth, young adult, adult, senior)?

Select members to be apart of the band who will respect the music that they have to play. In order to do so, each member would have to be versatile in being able to play different styles of music.

4. What would you deem important qualifications for a music director at a church of any size?

One of the most important qualifications of a music director is the ability to interact with others (a music director can't have the respect of those they are not able to interact with). A music director must understand and work jointly according to the pastor's vision and know how to incorporate the music towards that, know and understand the timbre and move of the congregation, be one that has patience, know and understand the requirements of their position, be able to communicate and articulate with others, one that is not passive but has compassion for others at the same time, understand and know each element or entity of the music department, have no respect of persons, know how to delegate, have organizing and administration skills, understand budgets and know how to work within a budget, be able to adapt quickly, understand and know the appropriate timing of the music, etc.

5. How do you measure weekly successes?

I would measure the weekly success musically by identifying some questions. Did the service start on time? Did it end in a timely manner (especially if there is back to back service). Was the music prepared enough? How did the music effect the congregation praise and worship experience? Was the music appropriate? Did it feel like a performance or did the music and the presentation of it invoke participation? How was the flow of service? How did the audio flow also in conjunction with the music department? Was everything in place?

A. Christopher Morris, NFPT, CPT.
(Musical Director of Mississippi Blvd., 312-Fitness, Memphis, TN)

Finally the musical teams of Mississippi Boulevard have been the most unambiguously, creative musicians with whom I've had the pleasure of sharing in ministry. Please note, every individual in this capacity under my leadership, has been exceptional in their musical offerings. The Blvd. brand of excellence was built by the combined synergies of voice and instrument. The musical teams methodology and brilliance go much deeper than merely learning repertoire. Current and former musicians have been sensitive and simultaneously aggressive as needed, with stunning accompaniment skills. I deem it an honor and privilege to have shared in collaboration with the musical teams of the Blvd. #salute

1. What are the essential steps/processes for creating a "good to great" church band/instrumental ensemble?
- Find qualified musicians with high skillset/gifting/level of anointing
- Access the minstrel's Musical personality
- Find applicants who understand proper business ethics/ acumen as the church is a business
- Find applicants that display a Personal relationship with Christ
- Personal chemistry with Band mates
- Desire for long-term residency
- Desire to see the ministry (Church) flourish

2. What tactics do you utilize to accomplish a "unified" ensemble?

- Establish honest, open lines of communication
- Cover for each other musically
- Open encouragement and applause for when each band member deserves it for their production
- Everyone must expect high levels of consistent production from each other at each gathering
- Strengthen all musical weaknesses

3. How do you go about establishing a unit that serves as an accompaniment to varying assigned age church choirs (i.e. children, youth, young adult, adult, senior)? Discipleship

Find musicians that understand:

- Dynamics
- Intensity
- Individual and Overall Volume levels from a mixing perspective
- Replicating a song from its original arrangement

4. What would you deem important qualifications for a music director at a church of any size?

- Musical Integrity
- Passion
- Commitment
- Accountability
- Excellent communication skills
- Ability to bring all musical ideas to life

5. How do you measure weekly successes?

- Ask ourselves were we a "help or hindrance" to the flow of the service
- The fewer the items of observation, from a critique standpoint, from the Director of Worship, constitutes a success
- Ask ourselves did we help set the atmosphere for, ultimately, the Call to Discipleship

With great humility I can say that I've been blessed by God to be a part of a few churches where excellence is a high priority in the worship ministry including the area of the rhythm section (band). Rarely do you ever find strong individuals on each instrument. It's during these rare moments in destiny that congregants get to enjoy such an offering of instrumental praise at its best. Such a unit usually is found at churches where the budget affords them to do so. I submit that every Pastor and Director of Worship (Minister of Music) should build their band starting with the organist and drummer.

The ability to minister vocally while not being limited to an accompanist with subpar skills is in my opinion invaluable. While not discrediting the importance of character, work ethic, discipline, and timeliness; having highly skilled musicians are a dream come true.

I firmly believe that each church should invest in their music department and remember that we are to offer God a more excellent SACRIFICE of praise. In building a solid band I would suggest starting with hiring an organist with all the musical skills and work ethic necessary to produce your church sound. The other side of the coin is having a unit that understands musical camaraderie and plays as an ensemble and not in competition against each other. Having played in not only dynamic local church bands, I've also been fortunate enough to accompany and learn from icons of this century: Donald Lawrence, Kurt Carr, Daniel Weatherspoon, Cedric Thompson, Mike Bereal and the list goes on. It's under the musical leadership of these giants that I learned to be a role player. Bands where each musician has full clarity of their role within the unit, makes for I what I consider DYNASTY INSTRUMENTAL ENSEMBLES.

There are some instrumental units that have "highly skilled" individuals who don't play in sync with the overall team and cannot accompany vocalists. Such an atrocity is what I term a "train wreck." Let's honor God, and hone our craft accordingly for the Kingdom.

PLANNING WORSHIP/MAJOR EVENTS:

One of the things that I am most passionate about is planning for weekly worship, concerts and major events. As with creative types, I dream BIG. Most time, I have to pull back due to budget constraints, players involved, etc. However, for the most part, I've learned to bring my initial "go to" efforts to God, and trust His promise: *"In all thy ways acknowledge Him and He will direct your path."*

When planning a concert, start with the "end result" in mind. Put careful thought into planning your program. Give yourself a minimum of 6-8 months to plan, with the understanding that a few changes might occur. I must admit, I have moved with such intense passion before that I've hardly noticed the pace, intensity and successes experienced. That can be favorable, but often, it's not so favorable. If you pace yourself, you will have outward success and inward peace.

WORSHIP PLANNING:

Concerted effort and consistent prayerful planning is needed to ensure the success of weekly worship. I am a proponent of the need for weekly assessments with a diverse team of visionaries. If the Senior Pastoral leadership is clear about the goal of worship, then the designated Worship lead should schedule a time that the worship service(s) can be properly evaluated and updated accordingly. There is usually a question as to whom should be a part of this particular team. I suggest the following:

*Pastoral Team Leads
*Worship Leads
*Media and Communication Leads
*Choral Unit Leads (per designated Sunday)
*Usher and Greeters Leadership

The team can vary depending on the needs and the goals to be accomplished weekly. As for me, I follow stringent rubrics to create a thorough yet vibrantly informative meeting. I suggest the following tidbits that create a GOOD MEETING.

*Creative, thorough and PRINTED Agenda

*Select the Right People

*Leadership MUST be prepared

*Make sure a well ventilated and comfortable room temperature is selected

*Keep meetings concise when possible

*Weekly review action items to be completed (champions must be involved)

*Celebrate the TEAM weekly

*Establish times of next meetings or changes.

*Publish minutes and forward to team with assignments

Below you will see minutes prepared from our worship design meeting. It lists all of the vital components mentioned above:

Meeting Agenda		Worship Design Planning
Monday, March 29, 2016	Worship Suite	2:00 p.m.

<u>*Attendees:*</u> *Audrey Storks (minute-taker), Leo Davis, Callie Kearney, Pastor Woodard, Pastor Carner, Rev. Self, Tim Dortch, Jonathan Cross, Paul Claxton, Pastor Anderson*
<u>*Conference Callers:*</u> *Chris Morris, Kaylan Johnson,*
<u>*Next Meeting:*</u> *Monday, April 4, 2016*

AGENDA
Devotion –Dr. Leo H. Davis, Jr.
BLVD "U" CLASSES – PASTOR BRANDON WOODARD
Will resume April 5th and April 6th
DEBRIEFING OF WORSHIP SERVICES FROM HOLY WEEK

Southwind: 9:00 a.m.		Midtown:	
Main Sanctuary – 386		*Main Sanctuary- 1805*	
Next Generation - 0		*Next Generation - 0*	
Discipletown Jr - 7		*Discipletown Jr. - 30*	
Discipletown - 0		*Discipletown - 0*	
TOTAL: 393	*2015 Average for March -259*	*TOTAL: 1835*	*2015 Average for March – 1219*
Guests- 13		*Guests- 65*	
New Disciples – 2		*New Disciples – 4 transfers and 1 baptism*	
Benediction: 10:05 a.m.		*Benediction: 12:10 p.m.*	
NEXUS Spring Fest – 1270+		*Good Friday – 1027; Benediction 2:35pm; Comments were*	
Families thoroughly enjoyed it		*shared from attendees regarding the 'touch of class' the Blvd exhibits from the hospitality to the selection of songs.*	

OBSERVATION FOR SOUTHWIND (Kaylan Johnson and others)

<u>Maundy Thursday:</u>
Benediction 7:05pm; Attendance 158
W:
-*great service* Comment: People spoke about it on Saturday during the SpringFest.
-*Smooth*
-*Loved the sermonettes* Comment: Hats off to Pastor Anderson for teaching after having dental work.
-*The purpose for communion and Maundy Thursday was amazing* -Music was soothing.
I:
-*we started late due to issues with sound.* Comment: We had a new mic for Pastor Turner that was being set-up.
-*Room set-up for Communion*
<u>9am service:</u>
Benediction at 10:05am
W:
-*great service*
-*Music was great.* Comment: Did not plan for the P&W team to sing during Communion. Choice of songs could've been at another level
-*Sermon was great*
I
-*crossroads was in sermon notes. Media left it up because it was there but had to quickly take it down* -mic wasn't working at the beginning
- *we didn't get the building open until 7:45, crew had the times mixed up.*
<u>12:30 service</u>
Benediction 1:32pm; Attendance - 107
W:
-*great service*
-*Music was great*
-*Sermon was great*
-*college kids seemed excited*
I:
- *finance crew wasn't back on time to collect offering* -security wasn't around when we were collecting offering Comment: Pastor Wood and Rev. Self will discuss an action plan moving forward.
- *very dark in the service* Comment: This particular service called for darkness; it went very well
-*The attire for the young ladies on the P&W team will be discussed among Dr. Davis, Paul Claxton and Pastor Carner.*
<u>**GUEST COMMENTS:**</u>
- *The word was fantastic; the play & dance was awesome; enjoyed the choir, sermon, & resurrection reenactment*
- *Enjoyed the Pastor's word, service & the choir. Everything was well put together & very entertaining.*

Meeting Agenda		Worship Design Planning
Monday, March 29, 2016	Worship Suite	2:00 p.m.

OBSERVATION FOR MIDTOWN (Ms. Diane Mayes)

Prep Rally: both 8:30 a.m. & 9:30 a.m. informative, discussing detailed logistics of all components of Worship in a timely manner.(Ministry representation: @ 9:30 a.m. **Today:** 1 = Elder, 1 = Diaconate, 2 = Ushers 0 = Greeter, 1 = Deaf Ministry.)

Prelude w/music: Prayer, Hospital, Recovering, Bereavement Lists, Screen Announcements began running on screens promptly @ 9:53 a.m. til 10:17 a.m. Media Ministry played music softly underneath.

Time To Talk With God: Beautifully set up by Pastor David Anderson. Prayer focuses were clearly outlined throughout & were presented on screens. Pastor Anderson led the Congregation in song..."Because He Lives". Ministers and the Elders met and prayed with Worshipers who came forth for prayer at the altar.

Sanctuary Chorus: entered the choir loft in orderly manner at 10:21 a.m. - beautifully arrayed in their "garments of praise"! Men in tan suits & bow ties...Ladies in beautiful dresses of pastel shades.

Call to Worship: Powerfully led by Pastor David Anderson @ 10:31 a.m. Great...uplifting, motivating **Call!!! "HE GOT UP!!!"**

Opening Song of Celebration: "Jesus Rose"...Beautiful song! Lyrics were presented on screens perfectly.

Litany: Beautifully done for **Resurrection Sunday!!!** Perfect presentation on the screens.

Praise and Worship: "Worth"& "That's Love"...Great job...David Edwards & **Sanctuary Chorus!!!** Sing Choir!!!

Prayer: Effectual prayer offered by Pastor David Anderson

Music Ministry: Sanctuary Chorus: "Crown Him Lord Of All"...absolutely beautiful anthem!!!(*Please note...the Media Team discovered, as the lyrics were being presented on the screens, that the lyrics that were submitted and displayed on the screens did not match the lyrics that the Choir was singing; therefore, after realizing this, no lyrics were presented for this selection.)

Worship and Creative Arts: "They Didn't Know"...absolutely powerful dramatization, dance, set to such a powerful message in song!!! GREAT JOB...ALL!!! Lyrics were presented perfectly on screens.

Powerful Preached Word: Pastor J. Lawrence Turner - "Never The Same Again"Mark 15:21 (ESV)....Powerful, Impactful Message!!! BIG IDEA: "Once you have an encounter with Christ and come into contact with His blood, you will never be the same again.""THANK YOU, JESUS!!! Most creative dynamic...preaching in the 3rd person as Simon, a Cyrenian! Thank you, Simon, for sharing a powerful Word from your perspective as you carried the cross!

Invitation to Discipleship: 6 came to JESUS today!!! "All of Heaven is rejoicing"!!! GLORY!!!!!!!
Communion: JESUS, THANK YOU for the invitation "To YOUR Table"!!! This do, in remembrance of Me."
"The Hill"...what a powerful word in song...powerful, David Edwards!!!

Media Ministry: The Worship experience flowed reverently, beautifully, seamlessly!!! No dead-spots!!!
Prayer, Hospital, Recovering and Bereavements lists, **The Litany, The Congregational Prayer,** screen announcements, song lyrics, video presentations, still shots...**PERFECT presentation** on screens, timely and accurate placements!!
Great job panning the cameras throughout the congregation!!!

Chapter 6

Meeting Agenda		Worship Design Planning
Monday, March 29, 2016	Worship Suite	2:00 p.m.

Plan Worship Service for 04.03.16

1- *Musical Guest – Alfred Ivery will minister in song at both locations (during the Communion) and offer his CD at a cost; Audrey will forward lyrics, a photo and mp3 file to Media and Communications.*

2- *Ushers/greeters/receptionist will seat, escort and direct guest to the appropriate areas at both locations.*

SERMON SERIES	MORE SECOND QUARTER DATES ARE FORTHCOMING
April 3rd- June 5th (tentatively) is a series entitled "10 Things" which is a shortened version of what initially started out as "10 Things I Wish Jesus Hadn't Said". This series focuses on some of the challenging and difficult sayings of Jesus and how we live them out as Christ's disciples.	*April 3: Installation of Pastor Virzola Law @ 4pm @ Lindenwood Christian Church*
	April 9: LeaderShift Meeting @SW from 9am-noon
April	*April 16: RHYTHM OF REST (No activities are scheduled)*
3 Matthew 5:10-11 "blessed are those who are persecuted"	*April 23: New Disciples Orientation @ MT from 9am-noon in the New Disciples' Suite*
10 Matthew 5:29-30 "if your right eye offends you…"	*April 30: Serve Tour (church-wide effort for outreach)*
17 Matthew 6:14-15 "if you do not forgive men their sins…"	
24 Matthew 6:24 "you cannot serve God and money…"	
May	
1 Matthew 7:1-5 "Judge not lest you be judged"	
8 Matthew 7:21-23 "Not everyone who says Lord, Lord"	
15 Matthew 16:24-26 "deny yourself…"	
22 Luke 6:24-26 "Woe to you who are rich…"	
29 Luke 6:27-36 "love your enemies…"	
June	
5 Luke 9:62 "No one puts their hands to the plow…"	

CHORAL UNIT ASSIGNMENTS FOR:

Southwind
April 3: Jiana Hunter and Praise Team
April 10: Substitute and Praise Team
April 17: Jiana Hunter and Praise Team
April 24: Chris Little and Praise Team

May 1: Jiana Hunter and Praise Team
May 8: Chris Little and Praise Team
May 15: Jiana Hunter and Praise Team
May 22: Chris Little and Praise Team
May 29: Jiana Hunter and Praise Team

Midtown:
April 3: Sanctuary Chorus
April 10: AOP & VOT
April 17: Sanctuary
April 24: MOPP

May 1: Central High School Chorus
May 8: AOP & VOT
May 15: Sanctuary Chorus
May 22: MOPP
May 29: Sanctuary Chorus

FOLLOW-UP / ACTION ITEMS

1. *Audrey Storks will contact Elder Peasant regarding assignments for Communion at both locations for all three (3) services.*
2. *Audrey will add new series logo to Planning center*
3. *Audrey will make adjustments to Planning center for all three (3) service based upon this meeting.*
4. *Pastor Woolard will provide baptismal candidates upon completion of classes.*
5. *Audrey will contact appropriate persons regarding the Musical guest for 4.3.16.*

How far in advance to prepare?

I've had to learn early on the importance of planning far enough in advance for ultimate success. That means dream big with as much information that you can gather up from the beginning. This will lessen the chance for those "uh-oh" moments. It's the "uh oh's" that kill the budget and the dream. Of course therein lies a contingency line, however with most churches we are operating with a "shoe string" start, and a hefty appetite and vision. It's safe to say for major events, I start sometimes a year out. Let's talk about certain facets of the planning:

Repertoire:

I am a strong proponent of storing up repertoire in advance (sometimes that means two to three years out). However, I will also place songs in a "future" folder and utilize them at the appropriate time. It's really about how to properly discern the season, the song, and our ability to make the music "come alive" in rehearsals and performance. There are seasons when a chorus is more attentive, more pliable to new experiences of music than others. I've become very sensitive to those milieus of time and space. My chorus tends to have high momentum after recess, (i.e. June and July) August through December. A brief two to three week break after their Christmas Concert, and full momentum from January through mid-May.

Repertoire choices have to be made and finalized six (6) months out due to the contractual agreements for orchestras that have to be in place. I must carefully sort out my repertoire choices. So, I'm constantly viewing and picking up repertoire for Christmas and other major High Holy Church Calendar dates, all year long. I think it's important to be open to all sorts of music (i.e. conferences, radio-npr classical, gospel, jazz, etc.). This will impact your planning significantly.

Anticipating Surprises:

Did I just chuckle aloud, from my memoirs of "SURPRISES?" Yes. I guess the question really stems from which end were the surprises coming—the visionary or the responsible cash disseminators? The lesson to be learned is this: careful, strategic, and methodical planning is critical to help lessen the surprises and to anticipate any unexpected situations that may surface.

> CAREFUL, STRATEGIC, AND METHODICAL PLANNING IS CRITICAL TO HELP LESSEN THE SURPRISES AND TO ANTICIPATE ANY UNEXPECTED SITUATIONS THAT MAY SURFACE.

Budget Dollars:

You have to know where the money is going to come from in order to support the vision of the event. To have vision without the monetary support, is like throwing your dream completely in the ocean never to be seen again. Will there be sponsorship? Will there be tickets to help defray the costs? Who will manage the ticket operation? Will the venue or church allow tickets to be sold at their location? Will the venue expect a percentage of the sales if you are an outside vendor? Costs of musical guests? Costs of added instrumentalists if needed? Cost of a hired arranger for orchestrations, if needed? A lot of these items come as bonuses or lesser costs due to "relationships" that I have built over the years.

Please note: It is of utmost importance how musical guests, or guests of any nature are treated and provided for when they are invited to share at your event. I have learned the importance of clarity of language on riders, what are the negotiables, while fully understanding all expectations appertaining to repertoire, attire, and accommodations. There are just so many facets to a successful concert that you have to start early in order to fully hash out all of the particulars. Some additional ancillary costs:

programs, lighting, extended stage needed, professional dance floor (if carpet is an issue). Is the pulpit/podium a "sacred area?" What are the variables involved? Are there outside personnel needed to supplement your program?

Date/Time/Venue:
Following budget dollars, the probable date, time and venue need to be secured as early as possible. It is imperative that calendars for church, as well as community, city and region are correlated to ensure no essential conflicts. I for one, had to learn with being in a smaller city as Memphis, that the Christmas season was widely celebrated by the community at large. Most times, there were conflicts with dates and times, which became added pressure to ensure that we coveted a good audience. I am adamant about rehearsing 6 -8 months out for an event, but I also recognize the importance of marketing. I fully understand and am aware that first, we work as unto the Lord, however your participants labor hard to sing and sometimes, they only end up singing to a half empty house. Here's the lesson: small things add up: prompt start and ending times, great music, great execution of music repertoire, diversity, adequate sound and lighting, etc. These are crucial determining factors on securing a solid audience-base for future events. Remember, it takes ONE TIME for a snafu and you will be labeled for the remainder of your career as a church musician. Please note, especially if your concert event is ticketed. You must be clear with all of the welcoming components of your church in particular. A marvelous program and performance can be marred for eternity because of someone's rude behavior (both ushers and greeters alike). Our customers expect top quality service when there is a cost associated. A wonderful quote from Malcolm Gladwell's *Tipping Point*: "Little Things Can Make a Big Difference."

Identifying partners?

When you have clarity with the Senior Pastor or Pastoral Team, the first group of "partners" to engage for the success of your concert/event would be: 1. planning

2. logistics 3. Sponsorships (as needed). Prayerfully select individuals who will support your vision and leadership. Not necessarily "yes" people, but rather persons who will credibly challenge or ask questions for the good of the organization, participants, and lead visionary. It took a long time for me to successfully locate a great support team and yet to fully follow through as well as build trust. One of the most significant groups needed especially if you are trying to locate sponsorship dollars to offset your costs, is to find a great personality and go-getter for Sponsorships. This should be an individual that is not a novice per se, but has some connections in the community to secure resources that will be validated and appropriate for your concert/event.

PLANNING DIVERSE REPERTOIRE?

I thought you'd never ask.....:) It took me a very brief moment in my career to identify solely where my gifts and passions lie. God has greatly given me the ability to fully engage a wide array of attendees for my concerts to enjoy wonderful diverse expressions of sacred music. I've learned that one's music should speak to ALL episodic adventures. Songs must be considered by the role they play in a specific context. I for one, was raised in a pretty diverse church cultural background, while both of my parents and grandparents were affiliated with the Church of God in Christ (Pentecostal), and there were strong African American Methodist Episcopal roots within my line of ancestral transcendence.

That being said, from my earlier documentation, my father's heart was that of a true musician. He wanted both of son's exposed to the best of the best of all genres as much as possible. Therefore, my introduction to diversity in sacred music was experienced well into my early to mid-teenage years. I was overwhelmed whenever I could experience any group or ensemble of African Americans singing anything outside of the sacred gospel music, while experiencing always jazz, blues and other African American art forms.

I recall my first concert as Director of Music at the age of 19 years of age. I programmed Wilhousky's, "Battle Hymn of the Republic," and Hall Johnson's arrangement of "I've Been Buked." Of course, I had not adequately learned or mastered the vocal technique, nuances, dialect, and/or appropriate styles for both, however there was an insatiable hunger to ensure that there had to be diverse programmings that satisfied my musical palate.

I'm approached by many musicians, who state that they are now employed at congregations, that don't necessarily sing hymns, anthems or spirituals, and the leadership would prefer that "those songs," not be utilized in context with the worship service. In fact many have sited to not be "word based," enough. As the kids would say, "side-stare.... pause." I'm not here to debate or settle cultural battles with belief or doctrinal differences. A brilliant text by Dr. C. Randall Bradley, *From Memory To Imagination* poignantly states: "The bible is clear regarding the Music We Should Use for Worship." There are two opinions that I want to clarify that Bradley's book brings to surface as it relates to executing music diversity:

1. Classically Trained Musicians Can Easily Adapt to Any Style of Music:

Many would like to believe that the aforementioned statement, however, is far from the truth when you try to categorize "ALL" trained musicians..... If you don't listen, expose and experience anything outside of a particular genre, how can you effectively communicate it or develop a passion for it? This goes for "Untrained" musicians as well. In order to experience, you have to be exposed first. I was exposed to the beauty of diverse music (i.e. anthems, spirituals, negro folk songs, traditional and contemporary gospel etc.) and extremely tasteful and poorly done performances. However, this gave me the opportunity to properly decide and chart my own intellectual path accordingly.

2. The Best Church Music Is That Created within the Church's Classical Tradition

If you take out Classical and fill in the blank_____ to describe your favorite musical tradition, I would respond, "how boring!" Too much of anything is absolute overindulgence!!! It is important to fully understand the culture of your audience and how to engage and educate them otherwise. That is a major task and it really takes allowing people to learn at their pace, and trust in the process.

I will say in the concert setting, there are prone to be outsider's attending (i.e. church and non-church), who really expect on some level a diverse program and then again, maybe not. I love the old adage, "give'em what they like, and shock'em with the other..." Only make sure that the "other" is qualitative and appropriate.

We recently collaborated with Mr. Larry Crawford and the Children Sing Production to pay homage and tribute to the life and music of Mr. Richard Smallwood. I was deemed the musical director for the event, and assumed responsibility for all of the music performed. Of course, this was a humongous and yet honorable assignment, which had to be studied very carefully. Richard Smallwood is noted for his interwoven abilities to carefully mesh the wonderful musical fabrics of classical and gospel into what I have called a "classpel" style. With that in mind, I prayerfully began to view the lists of artists secured by Mr. Crawford, and viewing the various videos and audio recordings, began to pull together a "favorites list" of Smallwood pieces. However, there was still the missing link for me. For a moment it really felt as if I was going to be on this lonely island by myself to decide if I would have to add other repertoire that was not composed by Smallwood. However, I stood on the premise that Richard was a classically trained pianist, and had a strong palate for a diverse musical program outside of his repertoire, mainly because of weekly experiences at the Metropolitan Baptist Church in Washington, D.C. He has served on the staff as artist in residence/pianist/member since 1985. Long story short, the diversity added simply made for a stronger implosion of worship as we shifted from one genre to the miraculous sounds and repertoire by Smallwood. For me, blended/diverse opportunities communicate well, and minister fully. For someone else, it might be a challenge. However, I've learned to respect where people are and to move on from there. God CAN be in it all!!!

Managing Choir Morale:
Ensuring that the choir's (participants) morale is consistently kept at a level that they are able to minister/perform at a high level and receive, is of utmost importance. The lives of those that we come in touch with from week to week and pastor, and teach, love, correct, etc. have become literal families to those of us whom we have been assigned. Outside of the rehearsal and performance setting, our lives are driven by so many distractions. Some distractions are good, some bad; however, it takes a prayerful and discerning leader to know how to keep the momentum of your choir in tact.

Those of us that lead have undoubtedly erred in this area, and often to the point where we have lost a few persons because of our overbearing tactics and rubrics. However, because of God's grace and love for us, I have learned the importance of how a "soft answer turns away wrath." As well, as "with loving kindness, I have drawn thee." This does not in no uncertain terms allow individuals to *do as they please,* but it does point to the significance of how "love really does cover a multitude of sins." People really don't want to know how much know, until they know how much you care.

PEOPLE REALLY DON'T WANT TO KNOW HOW MUCH KNOW, UNTIL THEY KNOW HOW MUCH YOU CARE.

Morale is really based on the energy, personality and preparation of the leadership. I have to creatively gauge, plan and implement weekly for rehearsals in order to keep the choir's morale consistently engaged for ministry The weight of it all falls upon the leadership (director), officers and section leaders (secondarily). As I stated earlier, organized, formulated, energized, innovative, engaging, informed rehearsals keep momentum and morale high, especially when spirituality is at the core of it all.

It's important not to allow things to fester or take root, (i.e. gossip, conflicts, etc.). I'm not necessarily for vent sessions, as I am for hearing from exactly what the word of God says about a particular issue and proceed from there. However, I deem it necessary to keep my ears always to the heartbeat of the chorus, to determine what needs to be a part of the conversation or dialogue with the chorus in special instances.

Ultimately, I live by these principles. If a chorus: 1. Enjoys the music and ministry of the chorus 2. Feels good about the music being rendered 3. Sings/Produces well …everything else will take care of itself, normally.

(PLANNING, POSSESSING, PREPPING, WITH POWER AND PASSION.)'

As I began to formulate this chapter through the initial outline, these words evolved as I thought about the essentials for success. I want to carefully detail each of these vital components for worship ministry:

Planning:

Planning for me is synonymous with constant and strategic research. My tendency is to carefully review most recent performances that carry the same weight of excellence. While reviewing, I am most cognizant of my goals and possibilities of stretching my gifts and talents as well as those I oversee. I'm in constant contact with those colleagues, who serve other congregations, university professors, or professional chorus masters and trainers alike.

Prepping:
Prepping in many aspects is synonymous to planning, with one exception: I believe there is more actualization required. Once I've planned, then I begin to actualize the plans by prepping. For instance, prepping for a Christmas Concert: there is the dissemination of a thorough rehearsal schedule, audio files, musical scores that must be processed and ordered. Prepping requires you to think on varied levels in order to be fully equipped for accomplishing the tasks ahead.

Possessing:
Usually as I move through the planning and prepping phases, I begin to take ownership of the process and visualize the successful outcome. To possess the vision is to
own every facet, which would include the outcome, whether successful or not. This also requires tough evaluation and feedback.

Passion:
When I've done the needful preparation, then I can **deliberately and passionately** deliver the results. Confidence is established as I appropriate the necessary processes of my planning, prepping and actualizing.

QUESTIONS FOR INTROSPECTION/
SMALL GROUP DISCUSSION

❶How does your team perceive your leadership? How are relationships "respectfully," being formulated? Are all team members held at the same level of accountability?

❷How do the instrumentalists that accompany your choirs function in their assignment? Are there regularly scheduled rehearsals outside of the chorus rehearsal? Do they function as a unit when ministering in worship? Are the musicians and chorus as one, when ministering or is there obvious competition?

❸Are there opportunities for you and your pastor, or team to discuss worship services prior and upcoming? If not, you can start small with just a weekly conversation with the pastor (i.e. time, flow, aesthetics, logistics, other needs), and build from there.

❹How do you begin the process of shifting the pastoral team, and congregation to deeper musical and spiritual appreciation; while remaining in line with the vision of the pastoral leadership?

❺How far in advance are you able to plan your musical repertoire for worship services? Are you holding all key leaders to the standard of excellence with repertoire choices that are appropriate to their assigned ensembles? Is their enough planning time for "theme based" worship" services that tie in or are relevant to the sermon?

CHAPTER 7
RELEVANCY: Evolving and Maturity

"Burnout is a condition in which a person's resource(s) of energy is depleted." - Hugh Ballou

Everyone wants to be relevant. Even the greatest among us, want to be known beyond the "good years." As musicians and worship directors, this desire for relevance can become obsessive. With shifts in leadership, musical preferences, audience demographics, the church is always changing. There was a time when every African-American church included congregational singing in their worship service. But that has changed. There was a time when choirs dominated the musical presentation during Sunday worship. But that has changed. As generations change, there is always a constant pressure and call to be relevant. By that I mean, it is important to communicate your gift through the medium of the age. This requires a great deal of contemplation, preparation, and relaxation. Without contemplation, you will never acquire the skills necessary to shift from one moment to the next. When you pray, you are seeking God's guidance on how to present your musical offering to the church in such a way that all who hear it will glorify God. When you research your area, you are also contemplating what is important for this community to connect and reach God. This is extremely important because when we do not do our homework, we end up only singing and playing songs that we like. And as a result, we lose our relevancy. As a result, we do not evolve with the movement of the church, and before we know it, we are no longer useful or asked to participate.

By preparation, I mean that we must always remain flexible. We must prepare for all stylistic musical presentations. I've shared this in previous chapters, but the key to my 26-year success has been, I believe, my versatility. I love all styles, sounds, and genres of music. I never allow my **resume** to stop me from learning. I cannot say this enough: if you do not make good on your preparation time, you will one day become insignificant. When we prepare musically, we are also preparing for a people who have yet to attend our church. We are preparing for grandparents who only come once a year. We are preparing for relatives who only attended because our church housed their loved ones' funeral. When we prepare for the people we see and the people we don't see, we open ourselves up to the glorious and limitless possibilities of God.

But not only should we have contemplation and preparation; but most of all, we must take time for relaxation. The chapter opened with an important quote that I may repeat again before this chapter ends. It's just that important. Hugh Ballou writes, "Burnout is a condition in which a person's resource of energy is depleted." As you aspire to remain relevant, remember that relevancy

RELEVANCY CANNOT HAPPEN WHEN YOU ARE NOT OPERATING IN RHYTHM.

cannot happen when you are not operating in rhythm. Relevancy can't happen when you're exhausted, frustrated, and overwhelmed. This is why, for this particular chapter, I want to spend a little time disclosing to you some of my personal battles. I want you to see that no matter how successful you are in public, if you don't take care of YOU in private, you will never enjoy the fruit of your labor. I have battled with depression and low self-esteem. I have battled with negative self-talk for a long time. But one thing I decided to do about five years ago, was counteract these negative thoughts with a positive affirmation of who I am in Christ Jesus. Within the last 5+ plus years, I've been able to ascertain a consistent rhythm for my life. As such, I've made a concerted effort to live in the moment. Naturally, as a planner, I am always thinking ahead. But sometimes, if you are not careful, you will accomplish something great and run directly into the next project without first celebrating what you accomplished.

To those who are like me, I want to encourage you to slow down and celebrate your achievements. If you don't, you will invite perpetual stress into your life, and anxiety will be your portion. I also want to recommend that you schedule your vacation time right after a wonderful event has taken place. After major events or concerts, I am more conscientious about my down time. In order for me to be refilled, it's important that I take the time to rejuvenate, rebuild, retool, and just plain do nothing for a number of days following. No debriefing, no conversation about what happened; I just decide to remove myself fully from all of the noise.

Part of the reason I do this is because I know myself, and the truth is you know yourself. In fact, nobody knows you better than you know you! And because I know myself, I know that I am an intense person (most creative people are). This means, I intuitively plan and execute my action items for a steady four to five months prior to an event. That's five months of thinking about songs. That's five months of talking to the guests. That's five months of corresponding with different administrators. That's five months of rehearsal and rehearsal preparation. That's five months of fundraising and decorating and designing and implementing and perfecting. The phone doesn't stop ringing for five months. The people don't stop pulling on me for five months. So, included in my planning of the event, is my intentional Sabbath time. Isn't that what the Father did when he created the world in six days? After He saw that it was all good, he took the seventh day to rest. God wasn't tired like we get tired; but I believe God did that in scripture to model what we should do in life. Never get so overworked by anything that it robs you of everything. Never allow people to see you out of character because of exhaustion or frustration. The enemy would love for you to be overworked because if the devil can't make you bad, he will make you busy. He will fill up your schedule with gigs and events and commitments that you can't keep; only to cause you to struggle with sleeping at night—and when you wake up, you're so cranky that nobody wants to be around you. Do you see that? Now, you've not only operated from imbalance and no rest, but you've also ruined your witness as a Christian. People know that you love God by the way you love them. If you don't take time to re-tool and refuel, then you'll never be able to love and lead from a place of overflow.

> NEVER GET SO OVERWORKED BY ANYTHING THAT IT ROBS YOU OF EVERYTHING.

This is why I'm taking the time to talk about relaxation in the context of relevancy. Both are interconnected. It takes a lot of work to do what you do. Why not pause for a moment, and embrace a season of rest? During that time, you can schedule intentional time to pray, retreat, replenish yourself, think, and pour back into people who have poured into you. As of recent, my best retreats are trying to get back as fast as I can around family, and my place of origination. I don't know about you, but it's something about being home with my family—good, bad or indifferent—that brings peace to my soul. If I am not home, there are specific places that I go to in order to retreat alone. During those moments, I take time to experience the inner me. I take time to examine my heart. I take time to worship the Lord and catch up on a good book or two. What do you enjoy doing during your "time off"? If you don't take time off, your body will do it for you. If you don't take time off, life will do it for you. That's why we have so many young musicians dying before their time. I believe it is because everybody told us how to perfect our gift, but nobody told us how to preserve our temple.

Scripture says, "Know ye not that your body is the temple of the holy spirit." That means, our body is the church. How we treat our body is how we treat our church. It would be hypocritical for us to lead people into worship in church, and not take the time to worship outside of church. When you take time to relax, you are more pleasant and easier to work with when you return. When you take time to relax, you'll also hear God more clearly and you can plan your next year with perspective and clarity.

I have learned the importance of rest and I'm glad I learned it now and not later. But I didn't learn it alone. My friend, Pastor Claudette Copeland, shared something with me many years ago, that I'm just really fully downloading in my life. "Leo," she said. "Always work out of the overflow, and you will never be depleted." I never quite understood that, nor how to effectively implement it, however now I see: she was talking about living a life in rhythm. When you live in the cyclic rhythm of seasons, you will work more fully and freely in the "overflow,' and you can refrain from burnout and depression; especially when a person suffers a loss of any type (i.e. spouse, family member, job, etc.). When this happens, there should be an intentional time built into your schedule to unplug and process what has happened. You've got to allow yourself to feel the pain, experience the grief, and heal. If you don't, you will bleed your unhealed wounds onto innocent bystanders who had no clue that you needed time to reflect.

We often place so much time denying our feelings that we actually convince ourselves that those feelings don't exist. But I've learned better. I now know that if I don't allow myself to grieve, then I don't allow myself to experience the attribute of God as a "comforter." God can't heal what I refuse to reveal. God can't rescue me if I never ask for help. He can't show up as strength if I don't admit I'm weak. It is my honest pain that God wants the most. It is my truth that makes me free. It is my brokenness that allows him to mend my heart. This has been the secret to my emotional success as it relates to my 26 years of ministry leadership at the Blvd. Despite all of the staff changes and philosophical shifts, I've been able to maintain my rhythm because I took seriously the most important tool to remaining relevant: relaxation.

What do you prioritize as a music director or worship pastor? Are you more caught up in the work of the Lord that you have no time to honor the Lord of the work? Do you find yourself raising your voice more often than you'd prefer? Does your ministry work honor God in excellence, and edify God's people? In my experience, it has been challenging to model and hold staff and volunteers accountable to this piece as it relates to replenishment. However, over time, people who come on board usually know prior to their arrival what the standards and expectations are and if they can measure up to them.

This brings me to another point about relevance. Where I currently serve, my staff is at least 15 to 20 years younger than I am. In order for us to work together, there must be a significant amount of give and take. What I'm grateful for is that this particular staff has taught me how to re-tool. I don't assume to know it all but I have also helped them to avoid making mistakes that I made when I first started out. So it works if you allow both generations to teach each other something. The younger staff members aid me in techniques and styles that I would not necessarily venture into finding out about, and I help them to remember the importance of a diverse musical repertoire and why that matters. They challenge me and I challenge them. In the end, God receives excellent worship.

CONQUERING YOUR OWN WEIGHTS

As you mature in ministry, you will mature in life as well. I am grateful for all that God has done through and in me, but I have not always been perfect. In many instances, I've held myself back on so many wonderful opportunities when I was 20 and 30, because of low self-esteem. During those years, I never felt that I was compatible, smart or worthy of anything beyond mediocre. I still don't know where exactly it all derived from, but that negative self-talk held me back for quite a while. Later it would continue because I was not actualizing or living a "life of rhythm." And now that I can see my life in retrospect, I think that part of my problem was that I was so focused on what I was about to do that I didn't look back to congratulate myself on what I had done. I was always looking at the things I did wrong, that I never celebrated myself for the things I did right. I was addicted to the problems, and I forgot about the purpose and the passion. Sometimes, in order to remain relevant, you've got to remind yourself of your purpose and passion on a consistent basis. After you've encouraged your staff or your team, you've got to take some time to encourage yourself.

You'd be surprised by how many people compromise their own success because of fear. You'd be surprised to know how many things I did not do that I wanted to try because I kept thinking about what others might say if I didn't do it well. But part of evolving is learning from your mistakes. You will never meet a successful person who didn't fail at something. But their failures helped them to get it right. Everyone has had a bad performance. Preachers have bad sermons. Singers miss a note or two. In life, the only way you don't mess up is if you are dead. And if you're alive, that means you have another chance to get it and do it right.

> YOU WILL NEVER MEET A SUCCESSFUL PERSON WHO DIDN'T FAIL AT SOMETHING. BUT THEIR FAILURES HELPED THEM TO GET IT RIGHT.

This is why, today, I often proclaim aloud when I feel discouragement setting in, "I can do all things through Christ who strengthens me" (Philippians 4:13). The simplicity of that declaration really works, and if you declare it, it will free you from the fear that is trying to control you. If you let fear control you, then negative self-talk will lead you right into the abyss of burnout. In my opinion, burnout is the tactic used by the enemy to thwart God's chosen plan for our lives. It dwells in the abyss of fatigue, depletion, vulnerability, and mental anguish. Burnout is a serious condition experienced by many in music leadership. Hugh Ballou states: "It has been classified as a 'condition in which a person's source(s) of energy is depleted." In other words, when you burnout, the flame that keeps our lives and work empowered is no longer burning. When you burnout, you set yourself up for living in what Shaun Saunders expresses as the Seven Deadly Weights that can oppress and suppress you: 1. Secrets 2. Insecurities 3. Worry 4. Comparison 5. Being Overwhelmed 6. Perfectionism. 7. Being Unprepared. These aren't sins necessarily, but if you allow them to, they will weigh you down and keep you from producing. If you allow them to, they will shift you into depression, low self-esteem, sleep disorders, missed deadlines, fatigue, compulsive behaviors, loss of confidence, and negative self-talk. Then, negative self-talk shifts you into lacking the ability to mobilize your thinking about the future, and once your future is compromised, then your faith is destroyed. If I am honest, I was experiencing all of the above, and yes, I was still a believer in Jesus Christ. However, I had to make a decision, and every day, I now make a concerted effort to shift from negative self-talk to positive solutions in my life.

So the big question is, what can be done? How can we evolve in our self-understanding even as we evolve as music directors and worship pastors? Firstly, know this: worship Pastors are constantly under the gun. We are scrutinized and evaluated at every public performance, worship service, rehearsal, and even in our personal lives. That is why we must take the time to take care of ourselves. The church is not obligated to do that for us. So below I have outlined a few suggestions to help you remain relevant and healthy as you grow toward a perpetual life of rhythm.

1. Take Time to Retreat- We as worship pastors never take enough time alone. We are bombarded by people, problem solving, creating for worship services, events, practice on a daily basis and fail to plan a time to retreat for spiritual and professional reflection. We must take intentional time to be alone with God, and with ourselves, in order to maintain excellence as worship pastors. Let me also add that there is absolutely no way to secure our success in ministry if we are not DAILY taking time to practice the presence of God. It is essential to the life of our ministry to do so. Long gone are the days of total reliance upon gifts, talents and resources. You will burn out in a matter of days from your own futile, human supply. At one time, I was fearful of the solitude, and what I might receive as a result. It sounds crazy, but it's true. I wondered if God would charge me with something so arbitrarily different or against my liking or standards. I would go so far, and move on quickly. Then I discovered that it was more about my personal discovery and need for his loving presence in my life. After I realized this, I began to cultivate a hunger for more of Him, which greatly aided my life.

2. Surround yourself with God-minded, and rhythmic living people. As the old adage says, "Birds of a feather, flock together." The scripture also dictates: "Do not be misled: bad company corrupts good character." It's vital that we are intentional about who we are surrounded by. I have become more cognizant about my conversations and surroundings, not in an effort to shun or make the appearance of me being so much better than, but I want to guard my life and my gifts. None of us want to end up in a pool of gossip and ruin our entire tenure because of the wrong group of people having access to us. Guard your life and guard your gift.

3. Have Fun! My goal is to educate and build up my participants, members of the congregation and community at large; however mainly, I WANT TO HAVE FUN... Music is not drudgery...it's fun! It's life! It's hope! It's unique! It's LOVE!!! I envelop it all and want it all. I enjoy it immensely, and I try as much as possible to stay away from anything that would take away from that joy. One of the triggers for me is anything that would try to lower the standard that I've been called to. That's not fun at all for me. This mindset helps me to keep my creative life evolving, my planning , etc.. If it's not fun, its drudgery and that takes me out of my life rhythm.

4. Remember, You are a Work in Progress. We're all a work in progress, but God placed us with all of the characteristics we have to make a better world and that is my endeavor. However, the key is that we recognize that God has designed us to do something specific for the kingdom that no one else can do. That keeps me grounded and conscious that it's not who can do it better or not; because I have been uniquely designed by God to complete a certain assignment, and I'm moving steadily forward.. I don't have to conform to what others think that my success should be or look like. My success should only be true to what I am and what I do. People would ask me all the time, "Why would you have a Doctorate and not teach college?" Well, because I love the work of the church and watching everyday lay people discover and make wonderful music, that is my calling. There is nothing more rewarding for me, than experiencing every day people being blessed and inspired by the music they experience. I had to settle with this conclusion in my spirit and remain constant to what I've been called to, and be resilient in my response to others about my call and purpose. My mantra is to *live my life and purpose, in rhythm and passion!!! I WIN!!*

5. Have more than one stream of income. Sometimes we can become so settled in our careers and one-sidedness that we think being a worship pastor is enough; not realizing that there is such a connection to many other avenues outside of being a worship pastor at your particular assigned congregation. I believe to a large extent my generation, relishes in the fact that there really is no need to delve outside. You can be successful in one place, we think. But I see it differently. Congregations are forever changing and the younger generations are utilizing every gift and talent available to earn additional streams. The question is, how does an individual calculate time for additional passions? It's called *organized planning*. I have done several things that have not only aided in additional streams of income but revitalized and rekindled my worship at a deeper level. It's all about gaining full clarity about the what. When you do that, then the where and the *how* will take shape.

QUESTIONS FOR INTROSPECTION/
SMALL GROUP DISCUSSION

❶Can you easily identify whether your current state is that of "burnout?" How have you managed or plan to manage to move beyond it?

❷Some creative types that I've experienced don't necessarily think it's important to take a respite or Sabbath, a few times a year. Or, they think just a brief weekend away suffices. What would you suppose as sufficient time and how to replenish? Is it important to add time of respite and rest in your personal and employment budgets? How important is it to plan what occurs during your time of rest and replenishment?

❸The seven "weights" identified by Mr. Shaun Saunders, are experienced in all of our lives at one time or another. How can one manage to at least be cognizant of the triggers that move us toward them? Is it possible to remain free and not experience those "weights?"

❹How important is it to have persons with whom we can honestly dialogue, who are not attached to our ministries? Is it O.K. to have accountability partners within proximity of what we do?

CHAPTER 8
Managing Conflict: *dealing with difficult people*

After all of these years of leading in music ministry, I am now sure of this truth: conflict is inevitable. No matter how nice you are, and no matter how spiritual you are, conflict is inevitable. Whenever you are dealing with more than one person who does not see what you see, how you see it, and why you see it, you will encounter conflict. But conflict isn't bad if you learn to manage it correctly. I'd dare say that a true leader is not proven until he or she is able to manage, resolve, and diffuse conflict. This is the test of your leadership abilities, because somehow, you've got to decide how much you will alter for others, how much you will remain obstinate about (without changing from your original position), and when to diffuse a situation because it doesn't help to major on a minor.

CONFLICT ISN'T BAD IF YOU LEARN TO MANAGE IT CORRECTLY.

I guess you can tell by now that I am an A-personality type. I like things done my way and I take time to execute a plan that will ensure every blindspot and tangential exception has been taken into consideration. *I guess that's also why I'm single. But anyway—that's another book, I guess.* From rehearsal to the final song, I have thought through every minute detail with sensitivity, discernment, and skillfulness. Even still, I will encounter someone who wants to do it another way. Even still, I will have to have a difficult conversation with a person who has decided to change the rules. Whether you realize it or not, your conflict management skills will make you or break you. What you say during a heated situation, is what people remember because you are the leader. You are the face that they see when they think music ministry at your church. Therefore, it is my hope that you will learn, through this chapter, how to manage conflict and how to handle problems, even if the main problem…is you.

Scripture says, "Where two or three are gathered in my name, I will be in the midst." I agree. I also believe where two or three people gather for any purpose, conflict will appear. This doesn't just happen in church, and we do ourselves a disservice when we over-spiritualize things that are not so spiritual. In corporations, there is conflict. In non-profit organizations, there is conflict. With family (especially with family), there is always conflict. In fact, you would think that people would stop their conflict during a wedding or a funeral just to get along for the cause, but all of us know these events can sometimes cause the worst conflict ever! So don't be afraid of it when it appears. Definitely go to God to get direction, but also, ascertain the necessary leadership skills to handle the situation as soon as possible.

Firstly, you must assess what kind of conflict this is. Jesus had conflict with his disciples. In the same chapter that Peter was elevated because of his revelation of Jesus as the Christ and the Messiah, that same chapter, Jesus rebukes Peter and tells him "get thee behind me, Satan." The hardest conflict to deal with is when you have to rebuke or correct someone that you just elevated. Why? Because they are helping you to accomplish a certain mission. You have put them in front of the people as your assistant or primary administrator. Then, when things go awry for whatever reason, you have to correct them in private without embarrassing them in public. Jesus knew that Peter had the right desires, but he was operating with the wrong motive. Jesus knew that he had to die on the cross, but Peter was, in that moment, being selfish. He didn't want Jesus to go because losing Jesus would mean losing his leader. Losing Jesus would mean his entire three-year journey was futile. Peter was in his feelings and Jesus confronted him, but didn't fire him.

Conflict doesn't always mean termination. Sometimes, you've got to train people into correction. Walk with them through the conflict, and monitor how they respond to moments when you disagree. Peter was a true follower of Jesus Christ. We know that because he stayed with Jesus even after Jesus rebuked him. You won't know who your true followers are until you have or encounter conflict. Judas, however, was a different breed. When Judas betrayed Jesus, that was indicative of something deeper. Judas had premeditated Jesus' demise. He had conspired against Jesus over time. He was in Jesus' face, doing what all of the disciples were doing, but his heart was far away from Jesus.

> YOU WON'T KNOW WHO YOUR TRUE FOLLOWERS ARE UNTIL YOU HAVE OR ENCOUNTER CONFLICT.

In life, you've got to differentiate the Judas's from the Peter's. Peter may have had a bad day. But Judas had a bad heart. If Jesus had gotten rid of Peter because of his bad day, he would've lost a significant apostle who turned the world upside down. He would've lost an evangelist who, with one sermon, converted 3,000 souls. Peter just had a bad day. When he denied Jesus, he was afraid of what life would be like without Christ to protect him. That's understandable. But Judas had a bad heart. Satan entered into Judas, and Judas, while under the influence of the enemy, sold Jesus for thirty pieces of silver. As a leader, you must differentiate your Judas from your Peter. You don't always know what

> IN LIFE, YOU'VE GOT TO DIFFERENTIATE THE JUDAS'S FROM THE PETER'S. PETER MAY HAVE HAD A BAD DAY. BUT JUDAS HAD A BAD HEART.

people are dealing with until they tell you. Make no assumptions. Assume the best but prepare for the worst. Ask direct questions. Tell them what you're noticing and attack the issue head-on. Don't participate in gossip. When it comes across your desk, call a meeting. Squash the issue as soon as you possibly can. Then, handle each person and situation accordingly.

If you have a Judas in your ministry, or on your team, you don't want them around anyway. But you have to continue to show the love of Christ until they resign; because trust me, they will resign. Jesus was willing to wash Judas's feet even though he knew that Judas would betray him. When Jesus got arrested, he looked at Judas and told him, "Whatever you're going to do, do it quickly." He never raised his voice. He never acted out of character. He still blessed those who cursed him, and prayed for those who despitefully used him. You've got to see this. The enemy wants to make you act out of character. He wants to cause you to experience humiliation in front of the very people who are influenced by your leadership. But you've got to operate in Christ-like love and conduct. Don't let Judas change who you are. Don't give Judas the satisfaction of your anger. Be angry, but do not sin. Pray that God will help you to confront Christ's way. If a situation is too much for you to do alone, consult an elder or a trusted spiritual authority to help you to diffuse the situation. Judas-like people need to be loved until they leave. Jesus never had to fire Judas because the love of God was so strong in him, that Judas eventually left himself. Your Judas will leave the more you learn to love like Jesus. And if firing is necessary, you still need to do it in a loving manner. Sometimes, people are wrestling and warring with their own surrender, and unbeknownst to them, they are taking their struggle out on you. God is dealing with them, but they haven't fully surrendered, so instead of saying, "Lord, help me," they, in turn, blame the very person that was called to help them through their situation. Don't trip over the small stuff. If Jesus was falsely accused, you will be too. If Jesus was mistreated, you will be mistreated, too. It's always about what you do with what happened to you, not necessarily what happened to you. Take TAKE THE PAIN OF THE SITUATION, AND TURN IT INTO PURPOSE. USE EVERY CONFLICTING ISSUE AS A LESSON FOR YOU TO BUILD UPON. the pain of the situation, and turn it into purpose. Use every conflicting issue as a lesson for you to build upon. Include, in your music ministry handbook, a written regulation in order to mitigate future instances like this. Don't waste any opportunities to get better as a leader.

Secondly, make sure that you obtain factual information. You'd be surprised to know how many ministries have lost their way due to false information. You'd be surprised to know how many choirs and music groups have disassembled their group because of rumor and conjecture. As a leader, you must ascertain truthful and factual information. You must vet the information and the source. Do not only respond to what someone said. If the source is questionable, get another source. If the information is questionable, ask for more information. Remember, "there are always two sides to every story; sometimes, three." We all have been dropped inside of a situation that had nothing to do with us. We've all been falsely accused about something. But as a leader, that's why you must document everything. Your character should speak for you. You should never put yourself in a compromising situation. With my staff members, I enjoy fellowshipping with them. With my choirs, I enjoy having a great time in rehearsals. But I am very clear with them: they are not my friends. I do not let my hair down with everyone because I have to maintain a level of respect worth following. I do not allow myself to be seen everywhere with everyone because Scripture says we must shun the very appearance of evil. You must get the facts. But you also must not allow people to have something on you that you wouldn't want others to know. Protect your testimony. Be a man or woman of integrity and character. Love the Lord in public and in private. If you do that, then you won't have to worry about being exposed. If you do that, then people will stick up for you even when others try to destroy you.

> WITH MY STAFF MEMBERS, I ENJOY FELLOWSHIPPING WITH THEM. WITH MY CHOIRS, I ENJOY HAVING A GREAT TIME IN REHEARSALS. BUT I AM VERY CLEAR WITH THEM: THEY ARE NOT MY FRIENDS.

Remember, the attack is great but the anointing is greater. The enemy wants to sift you as wheat, but if you make decisions to prevent the very appearance of evil, God will protect you. When you find yourself in a compromising situation, go to your senior leadership and tell them the truth. Sometimes, the issue is not that people have rumored about it. Sometimes, the issue is that they are telling the truth! They saw you at the event you shouldn't have been at. They have proof of your words through a text message or email. In this day of social media activity, you must protect your witness. You can't just speak to everyone offline without being aware that everyone has a recording device. Everyone has a phone and can snap

> IF YOU GUARD YOUR LIFE, YOU'LL NEVER HAVE TO RESIGN FOR SCANDAL.

a picture of text messages without you realizing it. If you guard your life, you'll never have to resign for scandal. If you live as if God is truly watching (the eyes of the Lord are in every place), then you'll never have to make a public statement of apology. Our lives are on constant display. Everyone sees us; whether we are out of town, in town, at a local restaurant, or in the privacy of our home. People have access to us now in ways that can compromise our entire ministry. When you go to conferences, think about your witness. When you go on vacation, think about your witness. All of us are trying our best to please God, and no one is perfect. But sometimes, situations can be avoided if and when we live out of a life of integrity.

Sometimes, conflict is only a symptom of a larger problem. Conflict with your team is bringing to light the areas that you need to strengthen. Maybe you are passive-aggressive and you have to learn how to proactively confront the situation before it becomes a problem. Maybe you have a tendency to set the bar higher than you can manage. Maybe you are not punctual, or you are too much of a perfectionist with others, but you are lazy and struggle with procrastination. Maybe this is a spiritual warfare issue, and you, as the leader, need to call a prayer meeting to diffuse the problem. Maybe there is a "cancer" in your ministry, and you've got to find the Achan in the camp so that your ministry can have victory (1 Chronicles 2).

If you are in a posture of prayer as the leader, and if you are in spiritual alignment with God, God will always expose the problem to you first before he allows it to metastasize in your ministry. You may not know what the issue is exactly, but if you pay attention to people, your spirit will immediately tell you when something isn't right. This is important, but many of us don't discuss the significance of spiritual sensitivity. Scripture says, "Be quick to hear and slow to speak." As ministry leader, you can't jump to conclusions. You've got to be willing to diagnose the problem, obtain the information, and then pray before you speak. That way, you will never have to retract or correct what you have fully investigated.

Thirdly, you've got to accept that some people must be loved from a distance. Proverbs 22:10 states, "Kick out the troublemakers and things will quiet down; you need a break from bickering and griping!"

(MSG) How do you love people who take advantage of you? How do you balance your life so other people's problems don't become your problems? There are two passages that teach us how to do just that: Luke 15:11-32 and Luke 10:25-37.

The story of the prodigal son (in Luke 15) is told after Jesus is accused of "welcoming sinners and eating with them." The story of the Good Samaritan (in Luke 10) is told after Jesus tells an expert in the law to love the Lord with all of his heart and love his neighbor as himself. Sarcastically, the expert asks, "who is my neighbor," and Jesus breaks out this parable to show us how to love from a Christ-centered perspective. Here is the take-away that I pray you will remember when the time comes for you to confront difficult, broken, or prodigal people: Love must be deliberate, but sometimes, love must be done from a distance.

When we hear sermons on the prodigal son, many preachers always talk about how the prodigal son demanded his inheritance, and how the father gave it to him. We always talk about how the son "came to himself" and how the father received him with love when he came home. What we don't talk about is how much love it took for the father to see his son walk away, in the wrong direction, and not go after him. The father exhibited not just love for his son, but trust in the God of his son's life, who was responsible for his son's soul. Sometimes, we love people in our ministries and on our staff to the point that we become blinded by over-protectiveness, and without realizing it, we get in God's way. Or, conversely, we are so smothered in fear that they will leave our church or our group that we act out of our emotions instead of waiting on God

SOMETIMES, WE LOVE PEOPLE IN OUR MINISTRIES AND ON OUR STAFF TO THE POINT THAT WE BECOME BLINDED BY OVER-PROTECTIVENESS, AND WITHOUT REALIZING IT, WE GET IN GOD'S WAY.

for instructions. But this is a question I want you to think about: what if some people MUST go through a season of prodigality for a reason you may never understand? What if God is telling us to raise the standard of excellence by refusing to compromise the rules for the person we enjoy doing ministry with?

No matter how good a leader you are, it takes LOVE and TRUST not to get in God's way. It takes LOVE and TRUST to stay home, and pray for your prodigal member, musician, or friend, even though you're not sure where he is and what he's doing. Scripture says that the father stayed home. The father didn't send the son sermons by email. The father didn't send the police to look for the son. The father knew he would be back home eventually, so instead of wasting his time looking for a son who wanted to be lost, the father converted that energy elsewhere. Sometimes, people want to be lost and you are interrupting God's process of conversion by making them commit to something they don't want to commit to. Instead of worrying over the one disobedient person, spend more time cultivating a culture within your ministry that others will respect and revere. Remember that sometimes, God will call us to love people from a distance because our love, like time, is a limited resource. We only have so much to give, and if you give it to the prodigal son (who isn't even in your house), you forsake the people who are IN your house; you forsake the other musicians who are in your band. You've got to ask the Lord to help you love from a distance. Pray for God to give you a plan and some peace because right now, the prodigal son hasn't hit rock bottom yet. And until he or she comes to themselves, they will always take advantage of you. Meanwhile, your house is disheveled. Their dysfunction has become your dysfunction, and the gossip they started in the ministry doesn't compare to the peace they stole from you now that you can't sleep. You're always worried. You're overthinking. And that is not God's will. Trust says, "God, this member belongs to you and I can't lose my peace over someone who doesn't even know I'm up at night." Trust says, "let me pray from where I am, and trust that God will send angels to protect and people to correct." Remember, some people water. Some people plant. But God gives the increase. Whatever your role is, do that; and nothing more. Love from a distance.

The Samaritan story has a similar message embedded within the thread of the text. As leaders of music ministries and a Christians, we must always respond to broken people with immediate concern and care. We must always be willing to take the first step in providing assistance for the immediate needs of victims. But don't overlook this point: the Samaritan brings the injured individual to a hotel, pays for him to be taken care of, and then leaves. We must not get so distracted by the needs of the injured that we forsake our own. We have to pray for balance, so that God can use us to respond, but also so that people don't confuse us for God. Loving from a distance means we deliberately place boundaries in our lives so that God can get maximum glory. When you decide not to show up to work or rehearsal, at the expense of someone else's bad day, you are not operating in God's will for your life. That is not congregational care, that is spiritual incarceration. God wants us to love deliberately, but also, He wants us to love from a distance. He wants us to confront what we can change, and trust him to do what we can't. This takes work. This takes prayer. But if you don't control the situation, the situation will control you. No matter the conflict, we've got to be willing to go to God to get his direction and guidance. Maybe you are the prodigal child. Maybe you're going through a difficult season and you need some time to heal. Be honest with yourself enough to know when it's time to take a break.

If you don't, you will bleed your pain onto innocent bystanders, and it will create a mess. When your heart is clear, and your motives are right, God will lead you and guide you to all truth. He will help you to listen with your heart and not just with your head. He will give you the grace to forgive, and a plan to restore. Remember, God is the one who puts limitations on us so we can be balanced, sober, restored, and resourceful. Don't let anyone turn you into their ATM machine, welfare office, or misery accomplice. Instead, be the leader God has called you to be. Seek to understand, don't rush to judgment. Handle your own insecurities and be honest about people you may be jealous of. *Yes I said it.* If you're not giving someone else a solo because you think they can sing better than you, then the issue is you. If you're not allowing someone else to stand out because you think they will ruin your shine, then the issue is you. Be man or woman enough to own up to the moments when it's you, and be Christian enough to apologize to those you have wronged. For those who have wronged you, know that vengeance belongs to the Lord. God will repay. He will compensate you for your compassion, and what you do in secret, he will reward you openly.

QUESTIONS FOR INTROSPECTION/
SMALL GROUP DISCUSSION

❶Is there a problem if "constant" conflict exists in your ministry?

❷How willing are you to prayerfully ask the Holy Spirit about your part in the conflict?

❸Are you willing to take the lead and go to the person involved in the conflict with you, or involve a spiritual mediator to assist?

❹In our quest as leaders to "seek to understand" all involved in conflict, do we ensure that we are bringing our best selves (i.e. emotionally, spiritually, physically and mentally) to the forefront?

❺If our motives are pure, God will stand with us and fight for us. Not so much to prove us as winners but that all can be brought into a deeper relationship with Him. How has conflict developed you as a leader and your team members?

CHAPTER 9
Transitioning Out While Facing Reality

No matter how great you are in your field, and no matter how many years you've been doing what you've been doing, one day, you're going to have to transition. Whether by relocation for another position, retirement, or death, transition is a part of life. But few leaders in ministry prepare for a healthy transition. Perhaps we are in denial about our age. Perhaps we are so in love with our work that we just don't know how to let it go. Perhaps a part of who we are has become inextricably interwoven with what we do. But regardless of the reasons we have in our head, if we are going to be an effective leader, if we desire to create a legacy worth following, then we should prepare for transition. In this chapter, I want to discuss the most pertinent subjects to consider when you recognize, "it's time to go."

I can't say I have all of the answers. I, too, am experiencing the labor pains of transition as I write. Having been at the Blvd. for 26 years, I am grateful for the 5 pastors under which I have served. I also love my church and the history and legacy it has represented for so many years. But if I am honest, I can feel the Spirit of God preparing me for transition. I don't know when the transition will take place—it could be three years, five years, or next year—but when the Spirit of God speaks, I must obey.

That's the first step to preparing for transition: you be must open to the Spirit's guidance. Scripture says in Jeremiah, "For I know the plans I have for you, says the Lord." This is a powerful Scripture that many

Christians know, but few Christians apply. God is the planner. We are the participant in that plan. God knows the plans that he has for us. We don't always know the bigger picture or the great plan because we are not in charge of the plan; we are participants within it. When we confuse our role and try to be the planner instead of the participant, we pretend to be God. We try to take his job, and then we make him the participant in our plans. We want him to bless what He did not authorize. We want him to co-sign on a situation he did not will. This is the first important step to recognizing when and how you will transition. You've got to fully surrender control of your plans and your wants to God. God sees what we can't see. God knows what we don't know. Ultimately, we must trust, as his children, that His will for us is greater than our wants. Ultimately, we must believe that God's word is true, and whatever his plan is, it will work together for our good.

> ULTIMATELY, WE MUST BELIEVE THAT GOD'S WORD IS TRUE, AND WHATEVER HIS PLAN IS, IT WILL WORK TOGETHER FOR OUR GOOD.

Surrendering control is a requirement. Allowing the Spirit to guide you is a non-negotiable. Once I submitted to the Lord, God began to take me places I never thought I'd go. He began to introduce me to the right people at the right time. In fact, when I think about how I got to Mississippi Blvd., I know that God's hand was in it. I know that He divinely orchestrated some conversations to happen, and some people to be in certain positions, so I could enjoy a wonderful ministry position at one of the greatest churches in America—and I mean that. If God could orchestrate my history, then I know God will take care of my destiny. If God could put me in places that I couldn't put myself in before, then surely God will

> IF GOD COULD ORCHESTRATE MY HISTORY, THEN I KNOW GOD WILL TAKE CARE OF MY DESTINY.

handle this current situation.

Transition cannot happen without trust. Proverbs says, "Trust in the Lord with all thine heart; and lean not unto thine own understanding. In all of thy ways, acknowledge him and he shall direct thy path." I believe when you sustain a life of complete surrender and perpetual acknowledgement, you won't struggle like others struggle with big changes in your life. Because I am adamant about having daily devotional time with God, surrender has become a little easier for me. Everyday, I acknowledge God. Every concert I do, I acknowledge God. I ask the Lord what songs should I teach. I pray for wisdom about the guests I should invite. When writing this book, I started each chapter with prayer because I fervently believe that God is smarter than me. I fervently believe that when you acknowledge God in all of your ways, God will bless what you do, and will lead you and guide you into all truth. This is a fact. I know it to be true in my life. So, when you begin to pattern your life around a commitment to trust the Lord, transition will not be as difficult for you as it is for some. Faith says, "I believe God can." Trust says, "I know God will." In life and in ministry, God transitions us by graduating our faith to trust. He uses conflict (like we discussed in the previous chapter) and challenges to awaken us to the reality of something. Sometimes, conflict exposes the person who needs to leave. Other times, conflict exposes the fact that we need to leave.

And transition isn't bad. If you stayed too long in the last season, at the church God planted you in, you wouldn't be able to appreciate the new season and the new connections God has ordained for you. Transition helps you to realize that God uses us for his glory, and plants us in a certain environment for a season. Once our season is up, we become unusable and unnecessary. Once our season is up, we become ineffective. Worst of all, once our season is up, if we refuse to leave, we end up taking someone else's position who is graced to be there, for this particular season.

After you surrender and trust God with your desires and plans, then you've got to face reality. I've mentioned this several times in this book, but when I look at my current church staff, I can't deny reality. The majority of the staff and ministry leaders are half my age. They are fantastic leaders in their own right, but I stick out like a sore thumb in some meetings. I never feel undervalued and unappreciated, but the reality is, life is moving. People are growing. The church is evolving. It would be foolish of me to come to church every week and never face reality. In a few years, because of the vision of where the church is headed, fresh blood and new, revitalized energy will need to occupy the seat I currently hold. And I am O.K. with that. Because as God prepares you for transition, he also gives you new passions and new desires. Now that I'm facing reality, I'm also dreaming again about teaching in the academy. Now that I'm facing reality, I'm writing books so that I can travel and teach at seminars and help music ministries around the world to enhance their leadership structure. When you say "yes" to the transition, even before it shows up, you will allow God to show you new areas and new passions that you didn't even know you had.

> WHEN YOU SAY "YES" TO THE TRANSITION, EVEN BEFORE IT SHOWS UP, YOU WILL ALLOW GOD TO SHOW YOU NEW AREAS AND NEW PASSIONS THAT YOU DIDN'T EVEN KNOW YOU HAD.

Next, you must ask yourself constantly, "What is God saying?" I don't believe anything happens coincidently. I believe God does everything for a reason. When I hear sermons, and when I have seemingly random conversations, my spirit is always listening for God's directives.

I am always paying attention to common themes being spoken over the pulpit in different regions. I hear God through the lyrics of songs. As you prepare for transition, you've got to spend time honing in to the voice of God. *God will never push you out, without preparing you forward.* He did it with Abram. When God was ready to exalt, Abram, a voice came to him and said one word, "Go." God spoke, and Abram moved. God will never expect you to move without first giving you a word. He always gives us something that we can lean on for direction. Abram didn't know where he was going, but He knew that God said go. He didn't know why he was going, but he obeyed God anyway. The lesson here is simple: God is not obligated to tell us where, why, and how long. But if we place our trust in him, then as we go, he will show. As Abram left his place of familiarity, God began to show him the next layer of blessings. What if God is holding up blessings in your life because He's waiting for you to go? What if you're asking for the full sentence but God wants you to obey off of a single word?

When God wants to get your attention, you won't be able to deny that He is speaking. Everywhere you go, you will hear Him. Every person you speak to, you will Hear him. This is why you must incline your ear unto the Lord on a daily basis, and watch God prepare you for transition as he simultaneously prepares the place he has transitioned you into.

WHAT ABOUT RETIREMENT? COUNT UP THE COST

Spiritually, we know we must surrender to God. Prayerfully, we love the Lord enough to trust him with our entire lives—even moments of discomfort and transition. But after we have ingested the move spirituality, there are some natural things we must also consider. Luke 14:28 says, "Suppose one of you wants to build a tower. Won't you first sit down and estimate the cost to see if you have enough money to complete it?" As it is in Scripture, it is in life. Transition should not happen without counting up the cost. Naturally, there are some adjustments that have to be made. If your salary changes, you won't be able to live where you live forever and drive what you drive. If you move from one state to the next, you will need to know what the cost of living is. In transition, you figure out what really matters. Is a $45,000 Steinway piano really worth my sanity? Or should I sell it, put some money in savings, and have peace when things shift? Do I really need two cars, or should I downsize? What about my retirement plan? Am I struggling to let this job go because I am comfortable here? *Am I still excited about what I do, or am I just accustomed to the situation I am in?* These questions are important for you to ask and answer because the last thing God

WHEN YOU SAY "YES" TO THE TRANSITION, EVEN BEFORE IT SHOWS UP, YOU WILL ALLOW GOD TO SHOW YOU NEW AREAS AND NEW PASSIONS THAT YOU DIDN'T EVEN KNOW YOU HAD.

wants you to be, is comfortable. The moment we become comfortable in anything, God will change everything. Counting up the cost considers not just your finances, but your emotional and physical health. You may want to travel the world after you retire, but if you are not healthy physically, then you need to count up the cost. As you transition from one season to the next, eliminate the unnecessary. The same way that we all do spring cleaning when the season changes, we must do the same in life. De-clutter your heart and mind, and allow God to eliminate the things that have no value anymore. Remember, once we go home to be with the Lord, we can't take any of this stuff with us. What if transition has come to help you to let go of things you refuse to let go of?

Not only should we count up the cost financially, but what will our leaving mean for those connected to us emotionally? How do we prepare loved ones and family members to embrace, accept, and grieve our departure? Many ministries lose entire teams when one primary person leaves because the team was built on this one personality. But I believe, if Christ is the head of his church, the church shouldn't die if you die. The church should still be able to function. The music department should still be able to thrive. Certainly, you will have different leaders who have different philosophies and personalities, but no one person should make or break a ministry. If that is happening in your organization, then you are not doing transition right.

Already, I am looking at a few students who are in doctoral programs who may be interested in taking my position at the Blvd., and running with the vision of the house. Already, I am vetting people, in my own way, for future leadership positions because I know I won't be around forever. In order for you to transition without casualty, you need to transition before you transition. You need to start backing up from being the only person they hear, and allow other people's voices to be heard. Many churches go into culture shock and trauma when their pastor suddenly expires without warning, because there was no system in place to account for transition. To prevent this from happening in your ministry, plan ahead. Include younger voices at the table so that your organization doesn't expire when you retire. Be open for God to shift your perspective and purview as He prepares you for transition. Embrace your limitations. Accept that the older one gets, the more set in his ways he becomes. Conquer the fear of flying. Don't worry about who will or won't hire you at your age. Trust in the Lord. God knows what you bring to the table, and if there is no room at the current table you are at, God will open up a new blessing that you have no room to receive. Pray more than you talk. Ask someone to discern with you. Resolve any conflicts that you may have with the pastor, staff, or members of the congregation. There is a difference between transition and termination. You certainly don't want your good to be evil spoken of. You don't want an argument to be the cause of your departure. The best kind of transition is one in which you don't burn the bridge that blessed you, because you never know who you will need again.

THE BEST KIND OF TRANSITION IS ONE IN WHICH YOU DON'T BURN THE BRIDGE THAT BLESSED YOU, BECAUSE YOU NEVER KNOW WHO YOU WILL NEED AGAIN.

Be open and honest with leadership about what you are sensing. The last thing an employer wants to hear is, "I got a new job and I'm leaving tomorrow." Like you, leaders need time to process, plan, and prepare for your replacement. When we make hasty decisions with transition, it shows that we do not respect the vision of the house. Give your leadership team time to train and build up the ministry before you leave them high and dry. These tips may be obvious to some, but you'd be surprised by how many people will leave their church for $20 more per week at the church down the street; and without warning, they are moving from church to church without proper, respectful, resignation plans in place. People won't always tell you the truth, but many skilled musicians and vocalists have been denied jobs because of their track record. As men and women of integrity, we must always be cognizant of our entry into ministry, and our departure from a ministry.

As I embrace another season of transition, I thought I would be extremely nervous about it, but now I have become invigorated. I am now able to dream again. I am now able to foster new relationships that have exposed me to multiple streams of income. I have true peace that God will take care of me. The money and the materials don't own me. If God has brought me this far, He will sustain me until the day He calls me home. This blessed assurance is the peace that I have which surpasses understanding. My prayer is that you will obtain that kind of peace as well. Everybody transitions. Eventually, you will, too. When Jesus was about to be arrested, he warned his disciples in John 14 that he was going to depart. They were sad. That is a realistic reaction to departure when someone has made a significant impact on your life. But Jesus told them, "if I don't go, then the Holy Spirit can't come." Jesus knew that so long as the disciples kept him around, the power of God would only be on them. But when he transitioned, the power of God would come and dwell in them. What if this transition is about God moving you from the power that is on you, to the power that will be in you? My word of encouragement is to trust God when you can't trace him. Believe him even when you want to pave your own plan. Remember, he is the planner. We are the participants. When we trust him with our lives, He will handle every season.

QUESTIONS FOR INTROSPECTION/
SMALL GROUP DISCUSSION

"Before making a decision to move, you must carefully and honestly evaluate your motives and reasons." Randall Bradley

❶If you are in the midst of transition or sensing the possibility of something altering in your current assignment; what do you sense God is saying? Are you creating space and time to hear His voice clearly, without distractions?

❷Are you feeling burned out or is it time to move on? Do you have wise counsel to assist you in discerning where you are and/or what stage you are in?

❸Are you satisfied in your present situation? Are you growing spiritually, musically, emotionally, etc.? What tools are you using to best assess your growth and/or spiritual maturity?

❹If you feel you have lack of support from the pastoral leadership team, or that you are being undermined, how can you best approach the situation without the possibility of termination? Can you honestly determine that you've fulfilled your duties at the optimum level of performance?

❺You can leave peacefully, if it's time. Devise your plan early and securely. Don't leave a job without a job!! THINK!!! What's the plan?

THE EPILOGUE

W riting this book, and expressing my heart on paper, has been one of the most daunting life assignments that I've ever accomplished. I never had the courage to communicate through written form—I was much more confident speaking about my life than writing about it—but one day, I realized: if I am to share vision with others, it must be written so that those who read it can run. The first of many books has been written. Now it's time for you to run with what you have learned, and change the world!

I hope you have gleaned from both my successes and failures in each chapter. At the end of the day, it's all about giving God the glory. Excellence can be achieved, if we are willing to throw away the tricks, gimmicks and games, and do ministry without excuse.

As a take-away, I want you to be encouraged to do what God has called you to do, even if it scares you. I want you to figure out why you are afraid, and then, lean in, trust God and do it anyway. I hope these final points of encouragement will move you from fear to faith; from trepidation to triumph; from doubt to destiny:

NO ONE SHOULD WANT MORE FOR YOU THAN YOU!
I'm so grateful for the support of my church family, the Mississippi Boulevard Christian Church, friends, family, and well-wishers. When I think about the many years I've served and traveled the country to speak as a clinician for so many churches near and far, one main question (framed

in many different ways) was always asked of me after each speaking event—it was a question I dreaded hearing until now: *do you have any product available? Where is your book with this information? How do we learn more about your successes at Mississippi Boulevard? We need to know more about the how's and why's of your projects? How do you see an idea come to fruition from its initial concept to final production?*

I always left my pleading audiences with the same old response, "I'm going to work on something." I believe that my initial invitation in 2008 to serve as Plenary speaker for the Hampton Minister's and Musician's Conference, is where I began to realize that my voice was important and documentation was needed. I just had no idea that my work was of value or valued enough by others. However, one day, I came face to face with the reality that I had to want it more than others; and until I wanted it more than others wanted it, it would never come to full fruition.

It's something about receiving all of the accolades from countless numbers of supporters, family members and well-wishers and still not believing that you can accomplish or make a significant contribution. I'm thrilled to say that I am so far beyond that point now, and it's primarily because I've come to realize that it's never been about me; it's about the Christ that lives and dwells in and through me! Once I made that discovery, then the "work" or rather, my self-sufficiency was not necessary. I learned how to REST in the finished work of the cross. That may sound strange, but it's true: in order to do what God has called you to do, you must develop a ready confidence and assurance that you are equipped, that you are able, and that it (whatever "it" may be) is already done because of Jesus' finished work at the cross!

STOP THE NEGATIVE SELF- TALK.

Next I had to move away from negative self-talk. I've mentioned this in several chapters in this book, but I could no longer make my success contingent upon other people's thoughts or feelings. I couldn't wait for outside validation. I had to learn to encourage myself. I had to learn to ask for help. I had to learn to confess what I wanted, and trust God to move on my behalf. In short, I had to exercise my faith. And in order to do so, I needed to change my speech. What are you saying about yourself? How do others experience you? Are you negative, pessimistic, and fearful? Do you always come up with an excuse before execution? Do you find it easier to encourage others, but you don't know how to encourage yourself? Speak life to your situation. Pray that God will remove doubt and fear, and then, begin to say what you want to see. You are successful. You are going to pass. You will achieve optimal success. You will recover. God is with you, and the more you believe that, the more likely your language will change about whatever you are hoping for.

I read a wonderful book by leading psychologist Tamar E. Chansky, PhD, author of *Freeing Yourself From Anxiety.* In it, she states, "Excessive self-criticism tends to backfire, because it leads us to focus on our so-called failures instead of the small ways that we could have improved." The constant replay of negative self-talk shifted me not only into low self-esteem, but it opened me to depression, weight shifts, etc. However, somewhere deep in the abyss of my darkness, there was always the glimmer of hope that would pull me through higher and higher until completely freed.

SUPPORT OTHERS AS YOU WANT TO BE SUPPORTED, REGARDLESS OF THEIR MOTIVES OR FEELINGS TOWARDS YOU.

When I began to support others despite their motive toward me, something amazing happened. The moment I put this principal into full practice, God started granting me unbelievable favor in ways I can not explain. My initial action plan was to make sure that my motives were pure. My secondary plan was to not look for reciprocity or mutual support, so that I wasn't disappointed when the people I supported didn't support me. Once I put those action items in place, I became exposed to resources and relationships that would ultimately help me to make my dreams come true. I was able to ask, see, listen, and learn from people I revered and modeled my ministry after. Scripture is true: you reap what you sow. Even if you don't reap where you sow, you will reap what you sow. Here's the lesson: support others, and watch God send support your way. Don't be selfish and stingy. If someone needs help, help them. If someone needs your presence, show up for them. God will never forget your labor of love, and he will reward those who diligently seek him.

> EVEN IF YOU DON'T REAP WHERE YOU SOW, YOU WILL REAP WHAT YOU SOW.

I am so grateful for those who supported me before I received this revelation. Their guidance and leadership helped me to obtain a healthy rhythm in life, and now, I'm experiencing positive outcomes because of their deposit. I have also been able to pay-it-forward by blessing my leadership team with the kind of honest and loyal support that I, by grace, have received from others.

BE THE BEST MODEL OF EXCELLENCE THAT YOU KNOW HOW TO BE.
DO YOU!!

The apostle Paul gives full awareness that we've been equipped fully for success: *"Blessed be the God and Father of our Lord Jesus Christ, who has blessed us with every spiritual blessing in the heavenly places in Christ."* Ephesians 1:3

According to the Word of God, we have been given everything needed to be successful in our passionate calls. As I've stated earlier, that's not to say that accomplishment will come without distractions or other deterrents. The realization of confidence can only come through God's word and presence, which must be practiced daily in our lives. If we rely on people to build us up, they will be quick to take us down when we are not valuable in their eyes. But if we put our hope in nothing less, than Jesus' blood and righteousness, we will be alright.

I often recite a wonderful quote that my dear friend would often share with me whenever I was discouraged. The quote is simple: *"Raise your expectation of God, and lower your expectation of man, and you won't be disappointed as much."* How powerful is that? I try to live by that motto, and when I am fully invested in expecting more from God and less from people, I am able to enjoy being the best model of excellence that God has called me to be.

Finally, we are all equipped to be originators of something great. This endeavor has now catapulted me to a new level of inspiration that I never saw coming! I can see my level of assignments changing, and I openly await all that God has. It's made me more empowered and assured that the success was not in my settling for the gimmicks or shortcuts, but rather, realizing that in His presence was where I could receive the ingenuity, creativity and power to accomplish anything imaginable. And you can, too.

In closing, I want to share with you one of my favorite passages of scriptures, my prayer for each of you accordingly:

May the God of hope fill you with all joy and peace in believing (through the experience of your faith) that by the power of the holy Spirit you will abound in hope and overflow with confidence in His promises. Romans 15:13 (AMP)

ACKNOWLEDGEMENTS

First and foremost, I am most grateful for the relationship with and guidance of the Holy Spirit. My continual process of learning to value and fully embrace my coveted daily prayer time and study of God's word have been my main ingredients for optimal direction and the successes in my life. "For I am not ashamed of the gospel of Christ: for it is the power of god unto salvation to every one that believeth... Romans 1:16

Special thanks to Mr. Shaun Saunders and the Godzchild Productions team for the thorough and supportive role played in the fruition of this project. Shaun, you kept pushing my thinking and writing skills to a much deeper level, and I am forever grateful. I am looking forward to the realization of the workbook (2017) and future endeavors with you and your stunning production team.

To the persons whose shoulders I stand upon, the late Ms. Grace Tichy, Dr. Charles Cleveland Clency and the Voices of Melody, Greater Galilee Baptist Church of Chicago, St. Luke C.O.G.I.C of Chicago, Martin Temple A.M.E. Zion Church, Charles Street A.M.E. of Roxbury, MA. Each of you have played a significant role in my development as musician and leader. I thank you.

Ms. Audrey Storks, my executive assistant, whom I introduce always as my right, left, hands and feet. She makes it all happen for me on a daily basis.

To the Mississippi Boulevard Christian Church (Disciples of Christ) congregation, I cannot express enough of my personal gratitude to God for placing such a dynamic spiritual family into my life. To the Pastors at The Blvd that I have served, learned and gleaned from: Rev. Dr. Alvin ONeal Jackson, Rev. Dr. Thomas L. Murray, Rev. Dr. Frank Anthony Thomas, Rev. Agnes Denise Bell, and our current and dynamic leader, Rev. J. Lawrence Turner. I am forever grateful for your trust and confidence in my gifts, and your spiritual leadership.

To all of my extended Memphis family members that have helped to hone and encourage me in ministry, Mr. Larry Crawford and the Childrens Sing Productions, the Celebration of the Arts Chorus, Mr. Michael Scott, members of the Memphis Symphony Orchestra and the many friends and well-wishers.

Friends, prayer partners, and well-wishers I could never have made it without. Mr. and Mrs. Clyde E. Hunt, Jr and family, Mrs. Sonia Louise Walker, Mrs. Joyce Blackmon, Mrs. Carolyn McGhee, Dr. and Mrs. Tyron Cooper, Mr. Brandon A. Boyd, Mr. A. Nathaniel Gumbs, Mr. Antonio Hunt, Mr. Brandon Waddles, Mr. Karlos Nichols, Mr. Braxton Shelley, Dr. Delesslyn A. Kennebrew (editor of life), Jermaine Manor, Pastor and Mrs. William Emmanuel, Mr. Lacy Brown, and the great cloud of witnesses…

BIOGRAPHY

Since the age of 15, Leo H. Davis, Jr. has served congregations bringing visionary leadership, structure, excellence, and the powerful display of music to the forefront for God's glory. A native of Chicago, Illinois, in which the vast musical exploits of the culture enveloped and birthed a unique musical presence in his life. He earned the Doctor of Musical Arts Degree in Church Music and Choral Conducting from the University of Memphis; a Master of Music in organ performance from the University of Massachusetts (Lowell); a Certificate from the Royal School of Church Music(Croydon); and a Bachelor of Music Degree from Roosevelt University (College of Music), Chicago.